Before Sunday

THE LIFE STORIES OF THE
BLOODY SUNDAY VICTIMS

22 March 2003

We sat next to each other in the Bloody Sunday Centre family room. Smoke circling, ashes strewn across the glass-topped coffee table, coats on to protect against dampness seeping from the old bank's walls. I sighed. Mickey smoked. We waited. I'd known Mickey for a year now and so, out of the silence, I finally asked the question I knew I needed to ask.

'Why do you look at me like you want something? You worked for six years to get the inquiry. What else could you want?'

'They were alive you know. Before he was murdered, my brother lived. Do you think you could write about their lives?'

Before Sunday

THE LIFE STORIES OF THE
BLOODY SUNDAY VICTIMS

For Keith & Virginia
"good old"
whose names shall
not be forgotten!
Happy every day

JENNIFER FAUS

NONSUCH

First published 2007

Nonsuch Publishing
73 Lower Leeson Street, Dublin 2, Ireland
www.nonsuch-publishing.com

Nonsuch Publishing is an imprint of NPI Media Group

British Library Cataloguing in Publication Data.
A catalogue record for this book is available from the British Library.

ISBN 978 1 84588 573 1

Typesetting and origination by NPI Media Group
Printed and bound in Great Britain

Contents

Acknowledgements 7

Foreword by Ivan Cooper 9

Background to Bloody Sunday 11

Johnny Johnston 19

Jim Wray 31

Gerald McKinney 39

John Young 57

Hugh Gilmour 73

Gerald Donaghey 87

Michael Kelly 105

Barney McGuigan 113

Kevin McElhinney 119

William McKinney 121

William Nash 135

Michael McDaid 149

Paddy Doherty 161

Jackie Duddy 169

Interviews 181

Afterword 183

Bibliography 187

Endnotes 189

Acknowledgements

Many thanks to Andrew Figgins, who assisted with graphics; Tom Mullen, who edited many early drafts; Patsy, who gave me a home at the Beech Hill Country House Hotel; the staff of American Airlines; the staff of the Tower Hotel; The Oak Grove and Mary B's for providing a local to a Yank; Catherine Duddy, Rhondalee Nash, and Hazel Donaldson who transcribed hours of interviews; and for their endless support thank you Lee Harold, Martin McCrossan, Matt Smucker, David Thompson, Steve Orth, Steve Anderegg, Paul Greengrass, Rhidian Bridge, Niall McCarthy, Vanessa Havel and Nancy Faus; and special thanks to Ivan Cooper. It would not have been possible without you.

For Wil, Emma, and Isabelle.

Foreword

On the third Saturday in January 1972, the North Derry Civil Rights Organisation held a protest march to Magilligan Internment Camp in Magilligan, Co. Derry. The march was to protest against the Special Powers Act, which enabled the Unionist Government in Northern Ireland to intern thousands without trial. In August 1971, internment without trial was used exclusively against the Catholic community. A number of those interned were no longer active members of the IRA. Many were selected because of their commitment to Irish history, the Irish language or Irish culture. In many instances, internees had been subjected to horrendous acts of brutality on the part of the Royal Ulster Constabulary, which was the police force.

One of the basic demands of the civil-rights movement was an end to internment without trial. Other issues, which were to mobilise thousands of people in Northern Ireland in 1968 and 1969, included 'one man, one vote'; an end to electoral gerrymandering; an end to religious discrimination, both in the construction and allocation of social housing and in public and private employment. The civil-rights movement had a strong commitment to non-violence.

John Hume, Paddy O'Hanlon and I, all civil-rights leaders who had taken our seats in parliament until internment without trial was used in August 1971, were at that march to Magilligan Internment Camp. There the marchers were confronted by Britain's Parachute Regiment, which was new to the Derry area. The regiment enthusiastically dished out harsh treatment to the marchers. Eight days later the regiment was used by the British Government at a civil-rights march in Derry, where they killed fourteen unarmed marchers, and injured double that number. That day is now known as 'Bloody Sunday'.

This tragedy was followed by a disgraceful whitewash inquiry, set up by the British Government, under the Lord Chief Justice of England and Wales, Lord Widgery – an inquiry which was subsequently proved to be seriously flawed. As a result of constant pressure from the families of those who died, and in an unprecedented move in British constitutional and legal history, another inquiry was set up. This one was headed by Lord Saville and is known as the Saville Inquiry, the outcome of which is still awaited.

I met Jennifer Faus, a Chicago attorney, five years ago as part of a group of Divinity postgraduate students from the USA to whom I was giving a talk on the civil-rights movement and Bloody Sunday. The daughter of ordained parents and a mother of three children, she was deeply moved by the events of Bloody Sunday and showed a special interest in those who had died on that day. Consequently she decided to write this book, a book which conveys a very touching insight into the personalities who were taken from us on Bloody Sunday. The events of that day were a watershed in terms of Irish contemporary history. Jennifer Faus, in this book, has personalised our loss. Her own sacrifices to complete the writing of this book have been enormous. Her commitment to the relatives of those who died has been unflinching.

Ivan Cooper, 2007

Background to Bloody Sunday

On 30 January 1972, the British Army deployed the 1st Parachute Regiment to conduct an arrest operation in Derry. But these were not arrest-operation type soldiers. The men of Britain's parachute regime are not ordinary soldiers. In their own words:

> They are firstly, all volunteers and are then toughened by hard physical training. As a result they have that infectious optimism and that offensive eagerness which comes from physical well-being. They have jumped from the skies and by doing so have conquered fear.
>
> Their duty lies in the van of battle: they are proud of their honour and have never failed in any task. They have the highest standards in all things, whether it be skills in battle or smartness in execution of all peacetime duties. They have shown themselves to be as tenacious and determined in defence as they are courageous in attack. They are in fact, men apart.
>
> Training is hard but it is really the easy bit; you can always give up in training – you can't give up in the bush. Recruit training in the Parachute Regiment is arguably the toughest and most professional in the world today. All instructors at the training establishments are amongst the best officers and non-commissioned officers from the Regiment. Training is hard, but it must be remembered that it is preparation for service in the finest Regiment in the British Army. It is achievable. However, you don't have to be superman to complete this training. All you need is guts and determination, and the desire to be a Paratrooper.[1]

In the words of Soldier 027,[2] a paratrooper attached as radioman with anti-tank platoon on Bloody Sunday:

Recruits for paratroop training are selected volunteers and in my case, of the fifty-six men who comprised the platoon at the start of training, fifteen of the original number marched out. Fifteen men all considerably stockier than six months earlier, able to run ten miles before breakfast without giving it a second thought. As with all human beings petty dislikes and ordinary friendships existed, but there was something more, an unspoken bond of pride, togetherness and professionalism.

This encompassed us all to the extent that it was what our lives were all about. Any group of men who have suffered humiliations and privations together, who have sweated and frozen together, but have always found that little bit extra to keep pushing on when others have fallen by the wayside, after weeks and seemingly interminable months of this finally to finish to reach the other side of the hill and have your efforts recognised in the symbolic form of a pair of "wings" and the coveted "red beret" will know what I mean.[3]

Why did Britain send her best men to arrest a bunch of 'Derry Young Hooligans'? Why were Britain's most coveted soldiers sent to scoop up a bunch of kids, from fifteen to twenty years old, who threw stones and bottles at the soldiers surrounding their neighbourhoods? Internment raids had swept hundreds of men from their homes. Wouldn't that method have worked just as well? Or what about scooping them up any other Saturday or Sunday when the young people were out pegging stones – when twenty thousand peace marchers weren't standing in the way?

Is there something in the history? On 24 August 1968, Northern Irish Nationalists marched from Coalisland to Dungannon and although police prevented the group from entering the town, the marchers succeeded in setting the Northern Ireland civil-rights movement into motion. This movement was rooted in decades of outrage against Unionist bigotry levied against Catholics, dating back to the Government of Ireland Act of 1920 that segregated Antrim, Armagh, Derry, Down, Fermanagh, and Tyrone County from the south's Dáil Éireann. The Stormont Parliament, Northern Ireland's ruling body, served the Protestant Unionist majority almost exclusively, while gerrymandering denied Derry's Catholic majority a voice in their government.

From the 1920s to the early 1960s, IRA violence tried but failed to provoke governmental change or secure citizen rights. The early '60s saw a decline in Nationalist support of the IRA and activity receded. Northern Irish were ready to test a new approach. The formation of the Northern Ireland Civil Rights Association (NICRA) was modelled on the civil-rights movement led by Dr Martin Luther King Jr in America, and set forth six clear demands:

- One man, one vote in local elections
- Removal of gerrymandered boundaries
- Anti-discrimination laws
- Fair allocation of public housing
- Repeal of the Special Powers Act
- Disbandment of the B Specials (An auxiliary police force, the B Specials were a part-time, Protestant militia that had been used occasionally since the founding of the state.)

The civil-rights movement gained momentum, with protestors consistently facing heavy-handed opposition from the RUC and other Unionist bodies. Northern Catholics had endured the RUC's brutality for decades. By the late sixties, a growing media interest in the Irish struggle for equal rights placed British policy in the international spotlight.

The civil-rights movement and the counter-effort set off violent tit-for-tat activities: Republicans set fire to Unionist leader Ronald Bunting's car, parked in Guildhall Square, as he rallied Unionist support inside. Apprentice Boys[4] marched along the walls bordering the Bogside, while students from Belfast marched through Unionist towns from Belfast to Derry. In response, Bogsiders taunted and pegged stones at the Apprentice Boys, and Loyalists diverted and abused civil-rights supporters along the entire route. In Derry City, RUC and Loyalists regularly injured marchers so as to discourage marches. At their extreme, the RUC beat Sammy Devenney so severely he died of internal injuries three months later. The Northern Ireland Civil Rights movement progressed as follows:

5 October 1968: RUC injures approximately one hundred protestors marching in Duke Street for civil rghts.

6-7 October: RUC – Nationalist clash continues. Derry's first petrol bombs thrown.

9 October: Students of Queen's University Belfast march against RUC brutality in Derry. Between 2,000 and 3,000 students participate, out of which the socialist organisation, the People's Democracy, is established.

9 October: Derry Citizens Action Committee (DCAC) debuts. Ivan Cooper (Protestant) serves as Chair and John Hume (Catholic) as Vice Chair.

19 October: 5,000 people attend DCAC sit-down protest in Guildhall Square. William McKinney is photographed sitting in the middle of the crowd.

16 November: 15,000 people re-enact the October 5th March. Minor clashes with Loyalists do not off-set the demonstrators.

22 November: Housing and local government reforms come to pass and Terence O'Neill, Northern Ireland's Prime Minister, makes an appeal for peace.

23 November: Stormont announces the abolition of the (Unionist) Derry Corporation and the appointment of a special commission to replace it. NICRA and DCAC follow with a self-imposed ban on marches.

1-4 January 1969: A turn for the worse: forty members of The People's Democracy march from Belfast to Derry. Despite Loyalist deterrence, the body grows to about 500. The RUC stands by while Loyalists attack the group. After two more assaults, the exhausted contingent reaches Guildhall Square.

4 January: The RUC breaks windows and assaults residents of the Bogside. Free Derry is born. Nationalists paint 'You Are Now Entering Free Derry' on the gable-end of a small house off Rossville Street, form protectionist forces, and build barricades.

19 April: Samuel Devenny is beaten by the RUC.

July: Derry Citizens Defence Association (DCDA) is formed to protect Bogside.

17 July: Sammy Devenny dies. 20,000 people attend his funeral, filmed by William McKinney.

10 August: The DCDA asks the Apprentice Boys to rethink marching along Bogside, but they refuse. Republican, Nationalist, and Labour leaders vow to defend the Bogside against Loyalist and RUC incursion. Women and children evacuate vulnerable areas, including Paddy Doherty's wife Eileen and their children who move from Hamilton Street, an incursion point, to Creggan Heights.

12 August: Apprentice Boys march on the edge of Bogside. Rioting breaks out. Three hours into the rioting the RUC breach the barricades and charge from Little James Street and Waterloo Place towards Rossville Street, the heart of the Bogside.

During 72 hours of constant battle, Britain uses CS gas in its own jurisdiction for the first time in history, firing 1,091 canisters and 14 grenades of gas into the Bogside. Citizens treat nearly 1,000 injuries in makeshift casualty units. All able-bodied men are called to fight. Erupting violence across the North causes over 500 women and children to flee over the border.

Irish Taoiseach Jack Lynch vows not to stand by while innocent people are 'injured or even worse' and requests a UN Peacekeeping force. Lynch sends Irish Army troops to the border to set up field hospitals. At 4:00 p.m. on 14 August, the British Army marches on Waterloo Place, bringing The Battle of the Bogside to an end.

Initially, the army and the Catholic population live in peace. Catholic women bring soldiers their tea and buns on china and offer warm drinks at night. Soon, however, Irish citizens regard the army as yet another instrument of oppressive British rule and the situation hits rock-bottom.

6 February 1971: The first British soldier of the conflict dies in Belfast.

8 July 1971: The army shoots and kills two young Catholic men, Seamus Cusack and Desmond Beatty. Official inquiry into their deaths is denied.

9 August 1971: British soldiers launch operation Demetrius: Internment.[5]

By 1971, nearly all of the civil-rights demands had been met. In other words, one man, one vote had been conceded, an end to electoral gerrymandering had been achieved, the Derry City Corporation (the old Unionist corporation) had been shelved and replaced by a commission. Legislation in relation to discrimination in employment and a points system with regard to the fair allocation of houses had been invoked. But one civil-rights demand was still outstanding, the focal point of the civil-rights movement, imprisonment without due process: internment.

Internment was a sore issue with the Irish-Catholic population. Used against them in the 1930s, '40s, '50s, and '60s, the official line of the government during those decades was that internment was used to curb IRA violence. Many people were interned, however, who had no connection with armed uprising. People who had an interest in Irish music and culture were likely to be interned. People who decided, because of their interest in the Irish language, to write their names in Irish, to be addressed in Irish, to speak the Irish language, were also lifted and interned.

Despite warnings from John Hume and other anti-Unionist politicians, in 1971 internment was again levied exclusively against the Catholic community. Elderly people and people with long-lapsed connections with the IRA comprised a large number of those scooped and interned at Magilligan Camp in County Derry.

On 9 August 1971, the largest and deadliest internment raids swept through Derry and Belfast. Internment meant being awakened before dawn to the din of garbage-can lids being banged on the streets, as women warned the men about the approaching military. Internment meant that no man in a Catholic household was safe. They could be removed at any time, without warning or justification, and held indefinitely. By the New Year, internment raids had swept more than 900 Derry men from their homes and families.

Reports of illegal interrogation techniques began to surface, including stories of sensory deprivation and beatings, a diet of bread and water, and being kept 'spread-eagle against a wall for up to sixteen hours at a stretch, always hooded and denied sleep while the roar of a jet engine drowned out the sound of everything else. They were beaten when they fell, then dragged before Special Branch officers for questioning before being sent back to the wall again'.[6]

Such interrogation techniques were based on the experiences of British soldiers who had been taken prisoner in the Korean War[7] and their use against interned Irishmen resulted in 'the United Kingdom being found guilty of inhuman and degrading treatment by the European Court of Human Rights'.[8] This court stopped short of declaring the use of these techniques torture. It begs the question: would the British soldiers captured in Korea say they were subjected to inhuman and degrading treatment, or, would they say they were tortured?

Ending internment through diplomatic and political channels was unsuccessful. Stormont would not budge on the issue. Cases at law were unsuccessful as the soldiers, granted broad powers of arrest, detention, and stop and search[9] effectively operated above the law. The people of Derry decided, therefore, it was necessary to bring international attention to the issue of internment. The non–violent civil-rights demonstration was their outlet.

Johnny Johnston

Johnny was a big man. He dressed well. How could a soldier from a distance from here to that house up there have missed him? Paratroopers who are trained, you know? How could they have mistaken him? [10]

To be the oldest victim shot on Bloody Sunday is a dubious honour. To be the only one not to die on 30 January, but five months after the fact. To be the postscript on every memorial, 'and John Johnston (59) who died later as a result of his injuries'. It might have been better to end with an unadorned grave in the city cemetery, unknown, forgotten. Indeed, if Johnny had taken one step differently on Bloody Sunday, anonymity would likely have been the result.

Had Johnny lived, he would have passed through his life like most of us – ordinary and forgotten. Johnny's life was unremarkable. He sold clothing, married late, never had children, drank, played cards, golfed. Likewise, most of us move though the world quiet and ordinary. But Johnny strayed from the pack and did an extraordinary thing.

With the exception of his brother-in-law John Duddy and Duddy's family, no one leaves flowers on Johnny's grave anymore. Johnny Johnston's family and friends are long dead. Johnny's father died tragically. While stepping onto the ferry that travelled from the Guildhall to the Waterside, he lost his footing, plunged into the river, and was drowned. No one remembers when Johnny's mother passed away or the circumstances of her death.

His brother-in-law knew only one of Johnny's siblings. Johnny kept no diary or journal. There are no surviving photos of his childhood. In 1946, at thirty-three years of age, he met, fell in love with, and married Margaret Duddy. Johnny's life is largely an enigma to us.

But the puzzle of his life becomes complex when we add the puzzle of his death. How does an old man, not participating in the 30 January civil-rights march, end up shot 200 yards away a full twenty minutes before the paratroopers opened fire on the crowd? Johnny and Damien Donaghy were standing on open ground. The shooters wounded Johnny and Damien only in the legs and arms. The shooters were just across the street, a distance of less than fifty yards. Why didn't they fire fatal wounds when they had ample opportunity?

On the last Sunday in January 1972, a bright, pleasant, crisp day, 20,000 men, women, and children assembled in Bishop's Field at the top of Creggan Heights. It was a carnival atmosphere as the crowd gathered. A lorry was placed at the head, followed by the 20,000 marchers, some of whom were singing the civil-rights song 'We Shall Overcome'. The march mirrored the civil-rights marches of the southern United States, and Martin Luther King Jr and Gandhi were the people the civil-rights activists in Derry looked to as their inspiration.

This march, the previous marches, and the entire civil-rights movement from 1968 in Northern Ireland, had been demanding the same rights as the people of London, Cardiff, Glasgow, and Birmingham. They were telling the British Government that if they were part of the United Kingdom, then they wanted precisely the same rights as the its other residents, who enjoyed due process, legal representation, and the right to trial by jury. Only after a trial and conviction in London, Cardiff, Glasgow, and Birmingham, was a person incarcerated. None of the men at Magilligan had been charged with a crime or afforded a trial.

After observing the morning deployment of a heavy body of troops on William Street, now known as Barrier 14, the march leaders decided there was no way the march was going to be permitted to proceed to the Guildhall. Chief Superintendent Lagan of the RUC advised the leaders that the army were very hard line. There was no question – they would not permit the march to proceed to the Guildhall Square. So the route was changed. At the apex of William and Rossville Streets, the lorry would turn to the right and drive along Rossville Street to Free Derry Corner where the meeting would be held.

It was accepted that some young people might break off and confront the army at Barrier 14. However, the bulk of the marchers would follow the lorry to hear the speeches. It was accepted that the march would not proceed to the Guildhall and Lagan was advised the civil-rights marchers would not attempt to proceed there. Lagan conveyed this information to the army. The IRA informed the march leaders they would stand down that day. The IRA confirmed no operations would take place on Sunday 30 January 1972.

At the apex of Rossville and William streets, the march, led by the lorry, went to the right, followed by most of the 20,000 people, singing civil-rights songs, chatting, holding banners and signs, enjoying their afternoon. However, a group of young men, intent on throwing stones at the army, were angry the march was not proceeding directly to the Guildhall Square and so they went down to Barrier 14.

After a bit of rioting – stone and bottle throwing, CS gas deployment, water-canon soaking, and many verbal exchanges between the army and a small contingent of marchers – they went their respective ways, the army back to patrolling Barricade 14 and the marchers toward Free Derry Corner for the speeches.

On 30 January, Johnny Johnston woke, dressed, had his breakfast, read the paper, and left the house to go sit with a friend. On the

way Johnny ducked gunfire to go to the aid of Damien Donaghy, shot by British soldiers. The time was 3.45 p.m, just over twenty minutes before the paratroopers stormed Rossville Street. In that moment Johnny became one of the keys to unlocking the army's claim that they came under attack, only returning fire on gunmen, nail bombers, and petrol bombers. In the moment he was shot, and through his subsequent death, Johnny's fate was sealed, he would not go quietly, ordinary, forgotten.

At the other end of the march, Barney McGuigan was shot at 16:20 as he went to the aid of Paddy Doherty. Johnny and Barney were fifty-nine and forty-one years old respectively; neither set out to participate in the march that day; both were 'old men' and would have been considered working men, family men, not brick-throwing young hooligans. But they weren't the only ones.

The twenty-eight people killed and wounded on Bloody Sunday were primarily young people. Eighteen of them were under thirty; of those, twelve were between the ages of fifteen and twenty. Six of the twenty-eight were between the ages of thirty-eight and fifty-nine.

In addition to Johnny and Barney, Alex Nash (51) was shot going to the aid of his son, William, murdered at the rubble barricade. His hands were raised over his head. Patrick Campbell (51) was shot as he sought shelter at Joseph's Place. Daniel McGowan (38) was shot as he helped the wounded Patrick Campbell to safety. Paddy O'Donnell (41) was shot when he threw himself down to protect Winifred O'Brien as the shooting began.

British Information Services in New York stated that the British Army fired only at identified targets – at attacking gunmen and bombers. This means that the six men listed above were gunned down intentionally. In the Saville Inquiry, Queen's Counsel, Mr Glasgow described a disciplined force as one that would unquestionably follow orders. Any breech of orders would be a matter of disciplinary investigation.[11] It follows then that if the paratroopers were a disciplined force, they would have followed orders without question and if they had breeched orders, they would have been subject to a disciplinary investigation. For their actions on Bloody Sunday, the soldiers' Commanding Officer was decorated by the Queen. How then, can we come to any other conclusion than that they were acting under orders to kill?

If the British Army had stayed within the framework and shot only the young men and boys, they might have gotten away with it. It is no secret that young men regularly engaged the army in stone-throwing and rioting. It is known in Belfast that young boys were luring soldiers into areas where IRA snipers lay in wait. In the latter half of 1971 the tension, especially in Belfast, between the army and the Irish citizens was escalating.

It would have been easy to lay the blame on the riotous hooligans. Plenty of footage shows them throwing bottles, rocks, bricks, anything they could get their hands on at Barrier 14 on the day of the march and nearly any other day after the army came in and the Bogside declared its independence. But they screwed up. The soldiers killed two old men and shot and wounded four others. Can it be true that Britain's best-trained soldiers could mistake tall, aging, balding men with a bit of a paunch for riotous teenagers?

And so, this ordinary man, Johnny Johnston, whose claims to fame were a mean hand of Whist and a penchant for whiskey, takes a stroll on a Sunday afternoon to sit with a friend and unravels the British Army. Is the ordinary, unlikely, reluctant hero sitting next to you in the coffee shop? If the bomb blasted would he carry you to safety? Would he stay with you so you wouldn't have to die alone? Would he step into the line of fire to offer you comfort and ultimately give his life? If so, would you have wanted people to know his name? And maybe something about him and his very ordinary life?

The E. Duddy Bar was in the original Bogside. Everything west of the walls from Strand Road to the flyover is the Bogside these days. But back then, Bogside Estate was a short stretch along the Lecky Road.

The bar on Bogside Street stood for five generations before progress intervened. Margaret was Eileen (E.) Duddy's sister. Johnny was the patron. At thirty-three, for the first time in his life, he was smitten. They met, fell in love, and were married, and for us, that's when Johnny's life begins.

Until he was married, Johnny worked as a salesman for McDevitts Drapery Business. He was good at his job as it seemed no one got out of the shop without buying something. Upon moving from the Waterside to the Bogside after his marriage to Margaret, he opened his own drapery (clothing) shop in the drawing room of the house attached to the bar. Delivering clothes and collecting payments weekly, his vans went into the country offering fashions to folks who could not get into the city.

Work, play, and home were all contained within the building: the bar and shop at street level and the five-bedroom house above. Situating his business next to the bar may not have been the best idea. Johnny enjoyed a drink and after a few years he closed his shop and went to work for Hassons on Ferryquay Street down the town.

Margaret worked in Bryce and Weston's shirt factory and looked after the house. Her sisters, Eileen and Lily, shared the house with Margaret and Johnny. Eileen ran the bar and Lily worked in the shirt factories. Johnny wasn't Margaret's first love, but it was her first marriage. Her first fiancé died of cancer before their wedding day. Margaret and Johnny didn't waste any time: they were married, skipped having children, and immediately set about enjoying their lives.

On a Sunday afternoon they could be found in the house playing Whist. A game of four players, two teams, it was won by counting cards, memorising what was played, and getting the most tricks. Johnny and Margaret also travelled as much as they could. Cobh in County Cork was a favourite destination as were Donegal and Galway.

In 1968, redevelopment, which had started up the hill in Creggan

Heights, reached the old Bogside. The E. Duddy Bar, home, and nearby houses, all built by Margaret's ancestors, were razed. Eileen, Lily, Johnny and Margaret bought a house at 50 Marlborough Street with the small compensation the city paid for the taking of their home, livelihood, and land.

Johnny felt the civil-rights campaign should be supported but only attended a meeting or two. The extent of Johnny's physical activity was a round of golf. His trophies still line the shelves at 50 Marlborough Street. He couldn't be bothered with marching, stone throwing, or rioting. Unless he could have been riding along in his car, Johnny wouldn't be attending any marches or rallies. Johnny thought the civil-rights movement ought to be supported, so long as he didn't have to put himself out to do it. He made a token effort, but a round of golf was the extent to which Johnny would walk.

However, on 30 January 1972, Johnny walked. He couldn't drive on account of the march. Johnny left the house and fell in with the march on Marlborough Terrace and on to William Street. He was on his way to sit with a man who lived near the meeting site. The man was a recluse and Johnny thought he might be nervous with all the activity. Johnny didn't get far. Midway down William Street, as he crossed a patch of waste ground, Johnny stopped to help Damien and was shot.

When John Duddy arrived at Altnagelvin Hospital, Johnny was sitting with the sleeve of his shirt and the leg of his trousers cut off.

He was injured in his right leg, left shoulder, and the back of his right hand. John thought it was odd that a man who panicked when he cut his finger at the house would be sitting up calmly talking after having been shot twice and rushed to casualty. But this was only the start of Johnny's strange behaviour.

He was never the same after Bloody Sunday. When he was shot he fell and hit his head, the injury causing a growth that put pressure on his brain. Johnny's mind started to wander. Once a good driver, he now ran off the road. Once the best salesman at Hassons, he began turning his customers away. Instead of talking his customers into things, he talked them out of them. Once able to count cards and memorise four hands at Whist, he started to forget things. He was confused.

Diagnosed with a subdural haematoma caused by the fall on Bloody Sunday, Johnny endured six months of headaches, confusion, epileptic fits, loss of speech, numbness in his arms, depression, and incontinence. In mid-May, he was sent to Royal Victoria Hospital in Belfast for an operation. His doctor noted that during his pre-surgical exam, Johnny was unable to give his history because of 'a drowsiness from which he can be roused but he is totally disoriented. His level of consciousness seems to fluctuate.'[12]

On 23 May, his doctor performed a right frontal lobectomy and removed part of the tumour. On 6 June 1972, Johnny's doctor described his situation as hopeless and transferred him to Altnagelvin in Derry. Johnny died on 16 June 1972. His wife followed him exactly fifteen months later.

In the days and weeks after Bloody Sunday, the media reported the paratroopers were engaged in a gun battle with the IRA. They couldn't have gotten it more wrong. When the British Army shoots Johnny Johnston (59), Barney McGuigan (41), Alex Nash (51), Patrick Campbell (51), Daniel McGowan (38), and Paddy O'Donnell (41), how can they stand by their accusations?

Johnny was a big man. He dressed well. He was mostly bald. He wouldn't have been described as youthful. So how could a highly trained soldier with a clear view from less than fifty yards have mistaken him for anything or anyone else? Why did they shoot Johnny?

John Duddy has a theory. A theory that is overwhelmingly supported by the citizens of the Bogside, Creggan, and Creggan Heights and brought to light in the Irish Government's Assessment. It is believed that the shots were fired in an effort to draw the IRA into the area and incite a gun battle.

Why Soldiers A and B chose to shoot Donaghy and Johnston remains a mystery. Don Mullan states that many believe these early shots, fired by support company of 1 Para and hitting Donaghy and Johnston, 'were aimed at drawing the IRA units down into the Bogside … the IRA reaction did not materialise … When the Paras moved into Rossville Street twenty minutes later, the fusillade of bombs and bullets they later claimed they encountered simply did not occur.'[13]

It is clear that the army approached the situation anticipating trouble. General Ford wrote a memo shortly after a visit to Derry on 7 January 1972, which reads, in part:

I visited Londonderry on Friday 7th January with ACC (Ops) and held discussions with Commander and Brigade, Commanding Officer the City Battalion (22 Lt AD Regt), and the Police Divisional Commander.

In the last two weeks there has been the usual daily yobbo activity in the William Street area and this has been combined with bombers making sorties into Great James Street and the Waterloo Place area. Neither foot nor mounted patrols now operate beyond the bend in William Street to the West of Waterloo Place as a regular feature of life. They claim that all foot patrols are put at risk from snipers in the Rossville Flats area.

In addition the vast majority of the people in the shopping area not only give no help to our patrols but, if they saw a youth with a very small bag which might contain a bomb, they would be likely to shield the youth's movements from the view of our patrols. We now have 52 men patrolling in this very small area constantly.

The IS (Intelligence Services) situation in Londonderry is one of armed gunmen dominating the Creggan and Bogside backed and protected by the vast majority of the population in these two areas, and of bombers and gunmen making occasional sorties out of these hardcore areas to cause incidents, mainly in the shopping areas of the Strand, William Street, and Great James Street.

The Londonderry situation is further complicated by one additional ingredient. This is the Derry Young Hooligans (DYH). Gangs of tough, teen-aged youths, permanently unemployed, have developed sophisticated tactics of brick and stone throwing; destruction and arson.

The weapons at our disposal – CS gas and baton rounds – are ineffective. I am coming to the conclusion that the minimum force necessary to achieve a restoration of law and order is to shoot selected ring leaders amongst the DYH, after clear warnings have been issued. I believe we would be justified in using 7.62mm but in view of the devastating effects of this weapon and the danger of rounds killing more than the person aimed at, I believe we must consider issuing rifles adapted to fire PV.22 inch ammunition to sufficient members of the unit dealing with this problem, to enable ring leaders to be engaged with this less lethal ammunition.[14]

We have also to face the possibility of a NICRA march from the

Creggan to the Guildhall Square at 1400 hours on Sunday 16th January 1972 (sic). This would be followed by a rally which will be addressed by Members of Parliament and leading members of NICRA. It is the opinion of the senior commanders in Londonderry, that if the march takes place, however good the intentions of NICRA may be, the DYH backed up by the gunmen will undoubtedly take over control at an early stage.[15]

A letter from Frank Lagan to the *Irish News* confirms that the army had been informed of the march leaders' intention to avoid confrontation with the army:

On Sunday 30 January 1972 a member of the NICRA[16] informed me that the march route had been changed in that the marchers would now go along William Street, turn right into Rossville Street and not come into contact with the army blockade.

I saw Brigadier MacLellan at his office at 2pm on that date. He was with General Ford. I advised these Officers of the message I had received from the NICRA member.[17]

But the army had been briefed. On 29 January, nine pages of restricted information[18] were distributed to twenty-five companies deployed in Derry for the march. This document shows the British Army believed it took 1,000 baton rounds, 1,000 CS containers, 400 CS grenades, 200 pairs of handcuffs, and hundreds of soldiers to police and monitor a peaceful civil-rights march. Coincidently, the briefing, made public through the Saville Inquiry, does not include the briefing the Paras received.

Johnny Johnston was a victim of that briefing and the actions of the soldiers who followed it. He became a martyr, when he set out that day simply to be a friend. His death stands as a silent testimony to what happens when armed soldiers decide to use helpless targets to provoke violence. It has taken thirty years, but the British cover-up has failed. No better evidence can be found than the death of Johnny Johnston – anonymous hero.

Jim Wray

My mother used to say, 'Jim, you don't fall in love –
you fall in love with love.
You fall in love with the idea of love.'[19]

There's a certain blessing in dying young. And that is that you never grow old. If you are lucky, and die young enough, you are never disappointed in love. No one has ever truly wronged you. You have hope for the future. You still believe you can do anything. You are fit. You haven't had the time or experiences that make you bitter, calloused, cynical, or indifferent. Because Jim never got the opportunity to grow old and become jaded, he not only left this world with joy, excitement, hope, and passion in his heart, he left those who knew him with that ray of light as well.

When Jim turned seventeen he began going to dances. It was his first foray into scouting for love. He attended an all-boys school so his first real smell, taste, and feel of girls came late. But his nights out gave his young sister Margaret an early glimpse into the teenage world.

Starry-eyed Margaret served coffee and tea to Jim and his friends after the dances at the weekends. She sat quietly listening to the stories the boys told about who they'd met out in the town that night, who they fancied, and who they didn't. Jim knew Margaret fancied one of the lads, but he just smiled and let her be.

'Jim would come in from work and say, 'I'm taking a walk down to so-and-so's house tonight. Do you want to take a walk?' Well that was just like an offer to go out. I felt wonderful walking out with him because he was a handsome strap of a fella. I'd be in school and people would say, "Is that your brother? He's beautiful!' I was so proud.[20]

Girls in the Wray house weren't to be let out until they were eighteen, but after two years of hearing all the details fifteen-year-old Margaret was desperate to go to a dance. Jim intervened with her father at the eleventh hour, volunteering to take her to the dance, stay outside, collect her, and bring her home. After some negotiation, her father relented and let Jim escort Margaret. The dance turned out to be the least exciting part of the evening.

'We came out of the dance, he met up with his friends, and the whole lot of us walked home. So then my girlfriends in school the next day were envious of me because it wasn't just my brother who walked me home!'

But Jim's kindness and generosity didn't stop there. It is almost as if Jim's love of the idea of love infused everything he touched, and everyone he knew, but that didn't mean it was appreciated – especially by Margaret's friends! If Mary talked to a boy at a dance, Jim would go over and say, 'Are you all right Mary? You having any problems?' The boy would take one look at the six-foot man staring down at him and go the other way! Which was fine if she didn't like the bloke, but if she liked him, it was, 'I hate you Jim Wray! I really do!'

'I hate you, Jim Wray!' was a refrain echoed by Margaret's friends throughout their teenage years. Jim lifted Mary and twirled her around every time he saw her in town in a short skirt. He scared them when they watched *Dracula* and *Frankenstein* on Saturday nights. He reminded them to be home on time and generally looked out for their well-being whether they liked it or not.

On 24 July 1971, Jim gave Margaret away. Her father said he didn't raise his daughters to give away, so Jim walked her down the aisle. As the family sat down to the wedding meal, news came to the house that young Damian Harkin had been killed: crushed by an army lorry, just outside in the car park.

Not typically one to riot, Jim nonetheless joined his brothers, all wearing their hired wedding suits, as they took out after the lorry. Photographs of Jim and Liam on top of the Saracen in the hired suits dubbed them the best-dressed rioters in Derry. But it was for the sake of young Damian that Jim took to the street that day. Damian had just gone to run a message for his mum in his own street and the army rammed him up against a wall.

'We couldn't just go on with the wedding could we? Just sit there and say "Naw, I'm about passive resistance." It was only times like that, that Jim went out to riot,' said Margaret. Otherwise Jim was a strong believer in gaining civil rights through peaceful means.

For example, Margaret was harassed daily by the soldiers on the walls as she went to and from work. They had a great view of her from on high and weren't shy with their opinions. It bothered Margaret but Jim bolstered her, 'Well! Aren't you good looking! Let them see that our Derry girls are gorgeous.'

At the same time, Jim worked the channels to do what he could to stop the harassment. He went to their father and said, 'The soldiers are shouting things at Margaret and other women that are not appropriate.' As a member of a liaison group between the army and the community, Mr Wray could send word to the officer to get his men to behave.

Reasoning it was better for the soldiers to keep their opinions quiet than for word to get to the fellas from the Bog who would not take kindly to their women being harassed, Jim saw a situation and tried to diffuse it. He wanted to avoid confrontation and settle things peacefully when he could. Jim Wray was a man who respected authority.

Jim's respect began at home. Jim's actions on one occasion solidified this for Margaret who recalls:

I remember when Jim, he must have been nineteen, came in for his lunch. My father was at one end of the fireplace, Jim was at the other, my mother was putting out the lunch, and I was futtering around. The conversation turned to a riot in the town that day. Jim turned around and said, 'The bastards!' My father got up and slapped him across the face. We weren't allowed to use bad language. I held my breath. Jim was taller than my father at that time and had he put his hand on my father, he would have dropped over. I thought, 'Oh God what's going to happen?'

Jim turned around and said, 'I'm sorry Daddy. I'm sorry Mammy. I'm sorry Margaret. I shouldn't have used that language.' I could not believe it. Any other fella of that age would have walked out of the house and said, 'I'm not coming back.' But it was my father's home, and Jim knew the rules. He broke one, took his punishment, and then apologised. Jim respected my father and my father's views.

But nowhere are Jim's beliefs more vividly expressed than in the photos of him on Bloody Sunday, conducting his own sit-down protest in the middle of the Barrier 14 riot. As the rioters pegged stones and the army spewed purple dye, Jim sat on the pavement in his dark cap, making his statement. He had said on more than one occasion, 'If we sit down, they won't run over us. Just sit down.'

Jim's love affair with the idea of love was clear, too. At twenty-two years of age, he'd been engaged three times. Engaged to an Israeli girl when he died, everyone thought this one would stick. She was beautiful, kind, and gentle. His family saw that she and Jim were very happy when they were together. They were waiting for permission from the Church when Jim was killed.

To marry a Jew, but still remain a Catholic, meant Jim would have to receive special dispensation from the church. So Jim and Miriam went to the local clergy and made their application. Then, at the beginning of January, 1972, Miriam went home to Israel to break the news to her parents that she wanted to marry a Christian. She asked Jim to go with her but he declined, 'Naw, I'm not going there for them to shoot me!'

Funny how things turn out. Jim didn't think he had anything to fear in Derry. He joked about getting shot in Israel. Instead, he was murdered in Glenfada Park. Witnessed by Joe Mahon who lay

wounded next to dying Willie McKinney and not fifteen feet from Jim. In his statement to Saville, Joe said:

> As I lay on my side my face was looking toward the North and I saw a Para walking toward the body of Jim Wray. This was the same Para I had seen [earlier] shooting from the hip. This Para appeared to be wearing a different coloured jacket to the other Paratroopers that I had seen that day. Although the jacket was green, its colour and markings seemed to stand out more than the jackets that the other Paratroopers were wearing. He was holding his rifle down by his hip with the muzzle down toward the ground, as if patrolling.
>
> He made no move to search Willie McKinney or me and effectively he walked in a direct line toward Jim Wray. He did not try and search Jim Wray or look for a weapon of any kind. He saw Jim Wray's shoulders move and realised he was still alive. The soldier then pointed the rifle at Jim Wray's back and fired two shots into his back at point-blank range. I could see Jim Wray's coat move twice.[21]

Liam and his uncle went to the morgue at Altnagelvin. Picking through the bodies, having to step over several lying on the floor, they found Jim on a trolley against the wall. He was cold. His eyes were open. Liam tried to close them. Jim's mother howled horrible chilling screams that haunted the neighbourhood. It seemed to her family from that moment on, she was never herself again. For nearly a year, she, Mrs Kelly, and Mrs Nash could usually be found in the City Cemetery or in the kitchen talking about their sons.

Mrs Wray died two years after Bloody Sunday, Mrs Nash seven years, and Mrs Kelly emerged from her grief in 1977 with no memory of the previous five years.

For Mrs Wray's family, the last two years she lived was time spent unwilling to let Jim die. It was Jim morning, noon, and night. She spoke to anyone who would listen, telling them how Jim was murdered, how the British military and media smeared his name saying he was a gunman, that her Jim would not take anybody's life! When she learned Jim was injured and murdered while lying on the ground, she was desperate to find answers to unanswerable questions, 'Between the first shot and the second shot, was he aware? Was he alive? Did he feel the pain? Did he pray? Did he think of me?' She tormented herself and everyone around her. Margaret said, 'We tried to bring her out of it. But she just wouldn't come back to us. We tried to get her to embrace her other sons. She said, "I love them, but what am I going to do without Jim? Jim's getting married. I have Jim's wedding money up the stairs. I have Jim's this and Jim's that." It was endless.'

Mrs Wray had not one moment's peace from the time she learned of Jim's death until the moment of her own death. The woman from whom Jim inherited his love of life, his love of love, sobbed endlessly. Angry and bitter, she raged at the world that took her Jim. She couldn't grieve and let him go and be the mother her other children needed and wanted.

But as much as she couldn't let go, the army wouldn't let her grieve. They raided the house relentlessly. They swept Jim's room time and time again. Mrs Wray insisted the house be spotless before anyone went to bed at night. 'They will not say our Jim came from a dirty house. Jim loved this house and when they come in here they will know what type of lad he was and they'll understand that they murdered a decent fella.'

Her health deteriorated. She didn't care about herself. She carried a great hatred against England and the British Army. Her family tried and tried to help, but they could not reach her. The children were devastated watching their mother deteriorate. But she slipped away from them, and were forced to go on without her.

Twenty-five years after her mother's death, Margaret organised a memorial Mass. At the evening meal, the siblings started to talk. Margaret shared memories of her mother:

'Our mother was always a very happy person. She loved being at home. On a good summer night she came into the street with us. If we were skipping, she skipped along with us. She showed us how to play hopscotch and how to play ball. When she was in the house doing her work, she sang. Even today, when I hear certain songs, I think, "Me mammy used to sing that!"

Our mother had great strength of character. She was the stability, the mainstay of our house, from greeting us at lunchtime to the minute we opened the front door always knowing what we were getting for dinner, she was in the middle of it all. Mother never went out because there was no need to – everybody came into our home. It never emptied. No matter what time of day or night, some cousin or some aunt or some uncle or some neighbour was sitting in the house talking to my mother as she worked, getting her advice or counsel.

Our mother was happiest with her children around her. She loved us wildly. She wanted us around so much we were never put to bed. We just fell asleep on the couch or the floor, and then our father or Jim picked us up and took us up to bed. Whenever anyone gave her a hard time about it, saying, "Your children need a proper bedtime",

she always replied, "I know where my children are tonight. Do you know where yours are?"

When she finished, Margaret's youngest brother, John, said, 'The woman you described and my mammy are two different people. You were talking about a woman that sang songs and laughed and skipped and played hopscotch and football. I remember a woman who was always crying and sad.'

Margaret realised the soldier did more than murder Jim and take her mother away. He also denied her young siblings a wonderful mother and brother. A mother and brother they never knew. Margaret has lovely memories, memories denied her younger brothers and sisters.

Jim didn't live long enough to be sullied by life. His idealism was never taken away from him. His passion was never denied him. He never had a bad back or a plump gut. Life never got a chance to corrupt or batter him about. He was just a good guy.

Jim's personal possessions on the day he died were a packet of cigarettes, 10p, and rosary beads. He didn't need money to enjoy himself. A walk out the road, a yarn with the lads, having a few jars on the Saturday night. That was Jim. Happy. In love with love. In love with life.

Gerald McKinney

Everyone makes choices. We choose to love and to forgive. That is the legacy that was passed to us from our parents.[22]

The McKinney family story is like a Greek tragedy. Act One is the story of Willie McKinney. He buried two wives and seven children. His third wife was twenty years his junior. Protestant blood runs through the clan. In grand patriarchal style, he was a clever man; a pragmatist; a business owner – one of few Catholics to own a shirt factory in Derry; and he lived into his '90s.

Act Two is the story of Gerry McKinney – James Gerald McKinney to be exact. William McKinney's third son, he was a suave devil-may-care fella who skated through life despite losing his beloved younger brother. Fred, Willie's fifth son, was killed in a car accident on his twenty-third birthday. Gerry belonged to the first genera-tion of educated working Derry men, and he took full advantage of this. An engineer, Gerry inherited his father's cleverness and ran several businesses throughout his career including a roller rink, a TV shop, an electrical business, and an engineering firm. Gerry married Ita O'Kane on 20 April 1960. He and Ita had seven children and were expecting their eighth when Gerry was murdered by British Paratroopers on 30 January 1972. Gerry was thirty-four years of age. James Gerald was born eight days after his father's death.

Act Three: Gerry's wife Ita struggles to raise her children while grieving for her murdered husband. She spends the first sixteen years calling her son Gerry, 'Baby', because she can't bring herself to call him by his father's name. Ita succeeds in raising her children to carry on their father's legacy – even though they were young when he died. All eight children share their father's traits, beliefs, and each has a piece of his personality. On 18 August 1999, Gerry is killed in a car accident on the Tobermore to Magherafelt Road. His wife is pregnant with their first child. On 18 July 2003, Gerry and Ita's second daughter, Regina, loses her husband to cancer while she is pregnant with their first child. In August 2003, James Gerald is born to Ita and Gerry's first son, Kevin, and his wife, Siobhan. He is the image of his grandfather.

When I started this project, I hoped readers would find someone with whom they identified. I discovered many families similar to my own. Of them all, Gerald McKinney's family reminded me time and time again of my own family. There were five boys in my dad's family: Jay, Bob, Glen, Hen, and Jerry. There were six McKinney boys: Louis, Laurence, Gerry, Denis, Fred and Willie.

After it nipped Gerry in the backside, the McKinney brothers locked the dog in, and lit the kennel on fire. Their da released the dog, it shot out and never returned. After it nipped Jerry in the backside, the Faus brothers lured the boar into the truck and drove it to market. The boar was not liberated by the Faus brothers' da.

The McKinney brothers painted the neighbour's dog green, white, and gold for the 12th of July. The Faus brothers sold a horse, trained to respond to whistles, to the neighbouring farm and then hid over the hill and whistled when the farmer tried to work the horse in the field.

The McKinney brothers broke into their own home, when their da locked them out to teach them a lesson. The Faus brothers blew a fifty-gallon milk bucket into the sky with a stick of dynamite they 'found'.

The McKinney brothers dug a hole in the garden to bury their nemesis neighbours, the Huey's. The Faus brothers tricked their nemesis neighbours, the Stauffer's, into sledding down a hill onto a not-so-frozen swamp. Their brothers would have you believe it was Laurence and Gerry of the McKinney clan and Bob and Glen of the Faus clan who were the instigators of it all. 'The two of 'em together, they were terrible,' was the accusation common to both families. I imagine, however, where four or five boys are gathered, trouble is not far behind.

Given the activities of all six boys, confession became part of the McKinney household routine, and Willie had a way of easing it out of them. Willie and Margaret had a knack for knowing everything

their sons were about, and there just wasn't any wriggling out of it. So eventually, under the skilled examination of their father, confessions typically resulted.

Over a bowl of porridge, for example, Willie might innocently ask his son, 'How did it go today?'

'Oh aye, good.'

'And the soap boxes were working OK?'

'Aye.'

'Had you a wee bit of bother there?'

'Nope.'

'I thought the wheels came off it.'

'Naw I fixed them.'

'Had you no bother at all?'

'No, but Archie had.'

'Oh. Did the wheels come off his?'

'Naw, he has a sore foot 'cause I hit him with the hammer.'

It didn't stop when the boys became young men. My father, Bob Faus, and Gerry McKinney shared the same smooth style: a cool confidence. When I think of my dad and Gerry, James Dean, Frank Sinatra, and Dean Martin come to mind – the cool guys – nothing rattled them.

When he came of age but still lived at home, Gerry stayed out until four in the morning and didn't apologise. Instead, in the morning, he sat at the table reading the paper.

'Where were you till half four in the morning?' His da demanded.

Gerry shook the paper and read on.

'I'm speaking to you. Where were you until half four in the morning?'

Gerry let the paper down. 'I was out enjoying myself.'

'You were up to no good.'

Gerry lifted the paper back up and went on reading.

'You were out till half four in the morning last night. What time are you planning to come in tonight?'

'Probably half four tomorrow morning.'

Is a person born with that kind of confidence or is it part of how he was raised? Gerry's parents were unique for their time in that Margaret was twenty years younger than her husband – scandalous in Derry. Also, there was no chastising in the house – instead, it was psychological motivation. 'It wasn't very nice what you did' or 'I don't think you should be proud of that' were phrases handed out by Willie and Margaret McKinney who also double-teamed their sons.

Willie went down the stairs to meet his late-coming sons while Margaret hollered down, 'Are they drunk? They better not be drunk! Are you taking care of this?' Willie shooed his sons up to bed, telling them they better hurry, they didn't want what their mother would dish out if she got to them. Of course, she never did. As the boys got older, the gauntlet was thrown down and their parents' strategy became more complex.

One of Willie's favourite games was the obstacle course. The boys only drank from eight till half ten when the pubs closed, but they stayed out 'sobering up' till the wee hours of the morning before sneaking back in to the house. Arriving home to find the gate locked, Fred said to Louis, 'Come on, I'll give you a lift up.' Gerry boosted Louis to the top of the fence, 'Jesus, Fred, Da's hooked a chain to the post and strung it across the garden and the car's parked underneath me!'

Gerry whispers up, 'Fall in on the roof of the car.' Louis fell. He crawls off the car and lets Gerry and Fred in the gate. By now every

dog in the neighbourhood is barking. They rest against the garden wall waiting for the light in their father's room but none appears.

Now it's Fred's turn. He raises the kitchen window and puts one leg through. He steps into the sink, does a contortionist move, and he's in. The sink's filled with water so he is wet up to his knees, but he opens the door for Gerry and Louis and they are in. They pause. No noise comes from the rooms upstairs. Gerry looks at Louis and Fred, 'Let's sit for a wee while and see.' They sit on the kitchen floor smoking, quietly chatting, and laughing about the night's craic. Twenty minutes pass. 'Let's try the door to the living room,' Louis suggests.

'Jesus, it's locked.' Fred turns to Gerry and Louis, 'Screw this!' The door breaks open with one swift kick. The room is dark, save for the red glow of their father's pipe, 'Ah, so youse have finally come home!'

Like the McKinney clan, my grandpa came from a family of sixteen children and my grandma from a family of eleven. That must be where they got their sense of humour and tolerance for raising five boys. After all, when you are one of sixteen, five might seem easy. I don't know where Margaret and Willie found their sense of humour together, especially in the face of so much tragedy, but maybe they enjoyed every day together because they knew the next wasn't promised.

Fixing dinner in the kitchen one evening, Margaret asked her husband, 'What's that racket out the back?'

'A goat.'

'A goat?'

'Aye, Margaret, it's a goat.'

'And just what are we doing with a goat?'

'Fresh milk, darlin'. Fresh milk.'

The next day the goat was let out. Margaret didn't know it was security given for the loan of a fiver, which at the time was a tidy sum for them to loan. From then on, whenever Margaret said, 'That milkman never came this morning! Louis, would you go to the shop for a bottle?' Willie responded, 'If you hadn't a let the goat out, you would have plenty of milk!'

Parental advice in the McKinney house always came with a bit of irony as well. One lesson Willie taught his sons went like this: 'If somebody asks you for money, just give it to them.'

'No, I don't believe that one, Da,' the son replied.

'Aye, it's true. But! Give them as little as possible.'

'I don't understand the logic in that.'

'It's very simple, if they ask you for a lot of money and you give them a lot of money you'll have to go try and get that back again and that is very difficult. But, if you lend them a little money and they don't pay you back, you can live without it. Either way, they won't come back and ask you for anything again.' Willie rested his case.

'Well Jesus, Da, that's a terrific plan so if I meet ten people on the Strand Road tomorrow morning …'

'You're exaggerating son. You'll only meet one at a time.'

Not only did Willie and Margaret subscribe to a somewhat different parenting philosophy from their peers, they showed affection in front of their children! Louis remembers his mother telling him she loved his father, saying, 'Oh my, he's a fine man.' Louis was shocked. Parents just didn't share stuff like that with their children. They loved each other! Imagine!

Even with six boys, there were occasional subtle, quiet moments in the McKinney house. Louis recalls springtime Sunday evenings

when his father played the piano in the sitting room, his mother hummed along in the kitchen, and Michael O'Hehir commentated Gaelic football on the radio. The smell of apple cakes and the occasional order, 'Get your feet off the mantle!' came from the kitchen to the boys as they lounged around, listening to the matches.

Gerry, Laurence, Fred, Dennis, Louis, and Willie in rare moments of silence, listening to football, 'Green Glens of Antrim' coming out of the sitting room, their mother singing, and a golden glow of sunshine casting shadows through the amber front-door glass 'is one of the nicest family memories I have,' Louis recalls. 'Back then, I never thought it would come to this, sitting here telling you about my murdered brother. I look at my life now and think, "I'm lucky. I've had a good run."'

Maybe it was the constant bustle of raising her own six boys and three stepchildren that made it go so fast, but to their mother it seemed no time at all before Margaret's boys were dating and then

married. Gerry met Ita when he was fifteen. Friday night was chaos. Six boys. One bathroom. Endless quarrels. Louis preferred getting punched up on the way into the bath than on the way out. He figured if you got punched going in you could clean yourself up. Cleverly, Gerry slipped in while the others argued. He sang as he washed and showered in a voice that rivalled mating cats and bad fan-belts. Gerry emerged with wavy hair, checked shirt, and smelling like a rose, as his brothers enjoyed pointing out.

Gerry didn't mind the ribbing once he met Ita. Ita O'Kane was a real doll, a catch, and after five short years of dating, she finally said yes, she'd marry him. Patience wasn't Gerry's virtue but Ita was worth it. She had blonde hair, a great figure, and whether it was her hand in his, her head on his shoulder, his arms around her waist, or their giddiness at seeing one another, she fit him and he fit her. 'Here ya go doll,' Gerry tossed his empty tea cup to Ita. In eleven years of marriage, she never missed. They were a couple. A perfect match.

Gerry helped Louis get married, too. When Gerry met Ita, he was absolutely certain she was the one. However, Louis found anxiety blocked his true feelings for Frances. On more than one occasion, Gerry approached the grieving Louis, 'What's wrong?'

'Nothing.'

'Do you want to talk about it?'

'Aye. But I'd need to trust the person.'

'Did you talk to Fred?'

'No.'

'Well, that's a good start.'

'What happened, Louis? You finish with your woman?'

'Aye, Gerry, we're through.'

'What did you do?'

'Nothing. We just fell out.'

'Well, Louis, if I were you, I'd be on that phone and talk to her and sort it out.'

'I'm not doing that. It wasn't my fault.'

'Oh, so you will lie there and break your heart hurting, but you won't apologise. Hmm. Where is she going tonight?'

'Jesus, Gerry, I don't know.'

'How do you know she's not sitting at home doing the same thing as you? Jump in the car. I'll take you over.'

'I'm not going.'

But Louis went. Gerry gave him a lift to Frances' house, and then Louis had to think of a plausible excuse for being there, which was usually something like, 'I just thought I'd come see what's the craic with you.' Frances was a forgiving sort and offered the olive branch, 'We're just going to the pictures. You wanna come along?' It's amazing Louis ever managed it, but he eventually asked her to marry him. However, it took Gerry to get him to the altar.

On his wedding day, Louis paced the floor muttering to himself, wringing his hands, and was just plain miserable looking when Gerry took him by the shoulders, looked him in the eye and said, 'Are you sure?' Louis replied, 'I don't know! Do I love her? Does she love me? I don't know!' Gerry said, 'Well, this is important. You've got to be sure! I've got a fast car out there. There's still time to get out. I'll take you away if you want to go.' It wasn't gentle but Gerry pushed the right button. Louis was forced to decide. Yes. He was sure. He pulled himself together, stood proudly, and married Frances. Forty-two years later he is still sure.

Gerry's first business was the Ritz. He'd met Ita at a dance there and when the owner wanted to retire, Gerry couldn't bear to see it close so he took it over. Dance halls were a dime a dozen, so he invested in skates and opened it as a roller rink. From the beginning, Gerry saw bigger possibilities in life.

One customer, an Englishman, had a beard and always came on his own. He drank the god-awful camp-coffee that cost 7 pence a bottle but made £2.50 in coffee; it was that thick. He skated round the rink at a slow, steady cadence. Night after night Gerry chatted him up. 'Jeff said to put a ring around the floor.' The next morning Gerry had a boy painting a ring around the floor. 'Jeff said to practice changing from right foot to left foot on the ring.' Gerry skated around the ring from right foot to left. 'Jeff said to get a partner.' Marie Kelly became Gerry's roller-dancing partner. Next, a sailor started skating around the ring and then another and then a few civilians and pretty soon Sunday nights were filled with roller-dancing enthusiasts.

The boys weren't out of the house long when Fred died. Fred's death was the first time Gerry's brothers saw Gerry slow down. The man who played cards for the fun of cheating at them, who never drove his car under ninety miles an hour, worked a full-time job, ran several businesses on the side, and had just married and started a family, finally slowed down. Gerry visited his mother every night, attending church with her and was devoted to her until his own death nine years later, but after a year of attending her every day she insisted he get on with his own life. He was alive, he had a family to raise, and she expected him to do it well.

Lawrence and Denis were away, so after Fred's death, Louis and Gerry became nearly inseparable. It was a natural, easy relationship. Gerry concocted the business promoting schemes in his head and Louis carried them out. One night at the rink, Gerry turned to Louis,

'It's a cold night isn't it.'

'Aye, it's cold.'

'See them soldiers standing out there?'

'Aye, Gerry, I see 'em.'

'I was thinking about bringing them in for a cup of coffee.'

'Jesus, Gerry, if your customers see them in here, they will leave.'

'We are warm and dry. They are cold and wet. Give them a nice cup of coffee and stand them in the corner.'

Louis went out but quickly returned, 'Gerry, the cops are there as well.'

'Bring them in, too.'

Louis went out again and approached the soldiers and police, 'Hello boys! Would ya like a wee cup of coffee?' They followed him in and Gerry told Louis, 'Go up there now and tell the girl to make the men coffee.' Louis rolled his eyes at Gerry but told the girl working the refreshment counter, 'See the guys in the corner? Give them coffee, Gerry said it's alright. And throw in some buns, too.' The girl replied, 'There's gonna be trouble.' But Louis was now onto the scheme, 'Naw, there'll be no trouble now, 'cause they're in!'

During Lent the dance halls were closed on Sunday nights. For a full six weeks there was no dancing on Sundays. Gerry saw not only a religious holiday but an opportunity to make money. It was easy to turn the roller-rink back into a dance hall once a week. But Louis saw trouble. Their mother attended Mass every morning and prayed the Stations of the Cross every evening. She might not approve of dancing on Sunday nights especially as it violated the wishes of the Church. Louis also thought, however, if they are opening on Sunday night, they should advertise, but Gerry said word of mouth would be enough. Nonetheless, on the Saturday before Lent, Gerry turned up in a van with a loudspeaker on top and pressed Louis into action.

'What are we doing?'

'You said we should advertise.'

'Jesus, Gerry, you said word of mouth!'

'It'll be words from yer mouth. Just say, "During Lent all dance halls are closed except the Ritz Ballroom run by Gerry McKinney!"'

The first Sunday they had 900 people at a half-crown a piece. When Gerry brought the money box into the house at the end of the week their mother was thrilled. Their father was wondering about the bumper crowd.

'You're marvellous! How did you get that?' he said. 'You only have seventy pairs of skates. You run it three nights a week and your normal takings is £45.'

'Well, we decided to open on Sunday for waltzes and foxtrots, you know, to keep people off the streets.'

'Really? Who's the band?' their mother enquired.

'Gay McIntyre Allstars', was the reply.

Gerry's parents were sure the priest would be coming down on him and there would be public outcry and then the police would get involved. It was sure to be a terrible mess. But for the next five Sundays, they packed the place. Gerry never had any trouble with the police. He'd been inviting them in out of the cold all winter for free coffee and buns.

Televisions were the next business target and once again Louis was along for the show. By this time, he was giving Gerry advice, which didn't mean Gerry took it.

'Gerry, that's the wrong place.'

'Why? What's wrong with it?'

'It's at the back of a women's shop. You have no shop windows. You can't sell TVs without displaying them in the window.'

'I'm not selling it that way, Louis. When we go round on debt collection, we can tell them to call up to the shop.'

'No man is going to walk through a woman's shop!'

'Louis, when they are walking in here, they are looking at the models. Besides, Derry women work. They'll be buying TVs too.'

The location of the shop proved no barrier to the sale of the TVs but Louis and Gerry had adventures trying to collect the payments. Once one-third of the price was paid, by law they couldn't repossess the set, so there was little incentive for folks to pay more than their third. Week after week Louis heard the same refrain, 'I can't pay you this week'. Back out at the truck he'd report, 'She has no money.' Definitely the brains (not the brawn) of the operation, Gerry would reply, 'That's alright. Jump in.'

Louis was the brawn and if any persuading needed to be done, he was your man. But, he was clever as well. At one house especially deep in arrears, Louis heard once again, 'I can't pay you this week.'

'Well, that's interesting. Gerry had to pay for it when he bought it. You bought it from Gerry, now it's your turn to pay for it.'

'Well,' the man dressed in a white suit replied, 'I can't pay you this week. Besides, this TV is rubbish; we shouldn't be paying for it.'

'What's wrong with it?'

'It's always flickering and blinking.'

'You want another one? We'll bring the new one in the morning. Would that be alright? Will you pay me then?'

'Aye, we'll pay you then.' Louis unplugged the set, took it in his arms and headed for the truck.

'Gerry! Open that door!'

'What are you doing?'

'It's a chance of a lifetime. They haven't paid us in three months. I am taking the TV. They told me to bring back another one in the morning. I'm not bringing them back a new one in the morning. They never paid us!'

'God almighty, Louis, that was a terrible low thing you done.'

'Nah, Gerry, not terrible bad; terrible clever.'

Even with the slow-payers and no-payers, Gerry's TV shop in Derry was a success. So successful in fact, he decided to open another shop. He hired a young man just out of school to run the shop. Louis argued against leaving a stranger in charge of the shop. But Gerry had faith.

Louis argued, 'He's gonna give everything away.'

'You're awfully cynical,' Gerry retorted, 'You'll see, he'll be a good guy.'

And he was right, the first week sales were good. The second week sales were good. The man sold TVs, sewing machines, portable radios. He was doing terrific. In the first month, sales reached an unheard of £1,000.

Out on their Friday collections, Louis worried the payments from the other shop were slow. He and Gerry finished their rounds in Derry early and headed over to ensure that week's payments had been collected. Louis knocked on the first door:

'Are you Mrs Doherty?'

'Aye.'

'I'm here to collect your payment.'

'Payment for what?'

'The TV.'

'Aye. That's the Doherty over there.'

And the next door: 'Are you Mrs Doherty?'

'Aye.'

'I'm here to collect your payment.'

'Payment for what?'

'The TV.'

'Aye. That's the Doherty over there.'

And the door after that: 'Are you Mrs Doherty?'

'Aye.'

'I'm here to collect your payment.'

'Payment for what?'

'The TV.'

'Aye. That's the Doherty over there.'

When he finally got back to the truck he told Gerry, 'There's ten Doherty's on this street. Your man has down Doherty with no addresses.'

'He sold a thousand pounds of merchandise. We've got to collect.'

'But Gerry, there's no addresses. What are we going to do?'

'I don't think there's a whole lot we can do. That's a terrible thing that guy done.'

'I told you he would give things away,' Louis reminded him.

'Aye. Put it down to bad experience. We'll go on.'

On they went. Gerry worked in Antrim, Strabane, Belfast, England, wherever he could get work that would teach him and further his skills. He trained in electronics, engineering, drafting, and architecture. The sophistication of his businesses increased. Louis found his own line of work and although the brothers had families to raise and their work lives were diverging, they met every Sunday morning to talk, 'I reckon I'm in this here because of you.' Gerry said to Louis about his work in engineering. 'Don't blame this on me,' Louis shot back. 'You told me to do what I am good at,' Gerry said.

The two talked about wives, and children, and bills, but mostly Gerry talked about the future, about his plans and grilled Louis, asking him what he thought. Louis often said to his brother, 'Why are you asking me? I don't bloody know much.' But he was honoured to be asked. Gerry was educated and exceedingly bright but he wanted to know what Louis thought, even if he didn't know anything about engineering. Louis' input mattered to Gerry and every week Gerry asked for it.

In Gerry and Ita's five years of dating, he brought her cigarettes and chocolate every time they went to the pictures. In eleven years of marriage he never stopped bringing her cigarettes and chocolate.

At thirty-four years of age, Gerry didn't get to fully develop his skills as a father and husband. In the early years, he travelled a lot for work. Driving to Belfast, an hour and a half each way with long and varied work hours made a daily commute impossible. In those days, Derry men had to go where the work was. A young husband and father, Gerry was away working for much of his children's early years, but he was fully present with his children when he was home.

Gerry's children took centre stage. He took them along on errands. He involved them. He gave them wee treats like a late night of football-watching with Kevin, or chocolate tea-cakes for Mairead as a toddler, who would manage to cover herself in chocolate from head to toe. Mornings when he was home, Gerry let Ita sleep, carrying a basket and tray to his children's rooms and waking them with tea and buns. He was strict with bedtimes and routine. His children knew what to expect. He was generous with love, affection, and praise. Gerry and Ita created a house of respect, love, affection, and fairness.

Her husband's death is a testament to Ita McKinney's strength and character. She raised eight children with no money, and they all turned out well. Her husband was murdered in the street yet she kept her family together. She lost her sole support and love of her life at the hands of another and she forgave. She taught her children to choose love and forgiveness over hate and revenge. She grieves and experiences intense sorrow for her husband and son, but Ita McKinney is a mother, wife, and woman: strong, resilient, and proud.

In the words of her daughter Regina:

> At the end of the day it all comes down to choice. I choose to let what has been done to affect me positively. I choose to want to make my daddy proud. I choose to be who I am with the circumstances I've been dealt. I choose not to go down the road that he was accused of. I choose to go down the road of forgiveness. I choose not to let my family down. Not to choose these things, to me, would dishonour my father's memory. I wouldn't wish on anybody what was done on us. When a soldier, police officer, or civilian is killed the person who shot him isn't hurting him – he is hurting that person's wife, children, parents, and friends.

Kevin was eleven years old when his father was murdered; Aileen, ten; Regina, nine; Tracy, eight; Martine, six; Fred, five; Mairead was eighteen months and then there was little Gerry junior – born eight days after his father's death.

At eleven years of age, Kevin was just starting to develop a more mature relationship with his father. They shared an interest in cars, sport, mechanics and engineering, an active lifestyle, curiosity, and a thirst for knowledge. On the morning of 30 January 1972, Kevin stood with his father in front of the hearth. Their backs against the warmth, Gerry's hands on Kevin's shoulders. Gerry had a new copy of 'Men Behind the Wire' and was playing it over and over again, singing the words to the song. Kevin can still recall the strength and pride he felt with his father's hands on his shoulders.

When Gerry joined the march that day, he was marching for civil rights. He wanted his children to have the same rights as Protestant children. For the wives of Derry men to rest well at night, not fearing their husbands would be abducted and interned. Gerry was shot while he and others attempted to take cover, fleeing from Glenfada into Abbey Park. His brother-in-law, John O'Kane, witnessed his murder:

> He walked forward onto the cobblestones and across them at a right angle, which led him on to the second of the three shallow steps. He was watching the alleyway all the time. As he approached the steps he turned his head to the left and put his hands in the air saying, 'No, no, don't shoot.' A shot rang out and he fell across the steps. He landed on his back and I remember him saying, 'Jesus, Jesus,' and blessing himself. The bullet had passed through his body, in one side and out of the other, from left to right; into the left chest under his armpit and out of his right chest under his armpit. He landed on his back. I remember seeing his coat moving as the bullet went through.[23]

After his father's death, Kevin was pushed into the role of man of the house, but at eleven years old he wasn't ready for the role. Nonetheless, he kept watch over his mother, learned to keep the house, pay bills, and mind his siblings. He wrapped his arms around Regina when she missed her daddy and needed to feel the protective warmth of a man's arms. He encouraged the young Gerry to take his first steps. He rebelled as a teen – fought with his mother and struggled to find his identity. He accidentally killed a wee lad who dashed out in front of his car and lives with the sorrow and pain that he is responsible for the loss of another parent's son as he raises his own five precious children.

He walked each of his sisters down the aisle. He carried his brother's coffin and walked beside his sister when she buried her husband. He calls into his mother since Gerry's death in 1999, just as his father called into his mother when her Fred was killed in 1963. Kevin McKinney is a kind and generous soul, and he and his wife have a house filled with love, respect, affection, and fairness.

Kevin and his father were only twenty-three years apart. By the time Kevin was twenty, had Gerry lived, they'd have been near enough like brothers. I think about my own son, just twenty years younger than I am and how much I enjoy him. I am thirty-five years old today and I can't imagine getting up, walking through Glenfada Park, and being killed. I would hate to miss the rest of our life together. There is so much yet to do. Kevin wishes his father had lived long enough to lift a few pints together, listen to Kevin's concerns, give advice, and, especially, to meet his grandchildren.

In August 2003, Kevin's wife gave birth to the third James Gerald McKinney. Perhaps in twenty years my son and I can return to Derry so we can all raise a glass to the first Gerry McKinney. For remembering him not only reminds us of a tragic injustice, it also testifies to the strength and character of a Derry family whose lives personify a legacy never to be forgotten.

John Young

I'd rather be the mother of a murdered son,
than the mother of a murderer.[24]

The air was unusually dry for a late January day in Derry. John woke at half seven and put on his new suit and the white shirt his mother had just bought from Graham Hunter's. The dark blue with a fine pinstripe looked sharp and professional. Specially made, John had designed the single-breasted, three-button suit with a narrow revere and raised the vent in the back. Not the style of the day; this was cutting edge. He always wanted to look his best, especially if girls were about, and with John Young, girls were always about.

> As I put the final touches on me look for the day – graduation ring on me right ring-finger, garnet ring on me left ring-finger, watch face-up on the thumb side of me left wrist, and me tie-pin, I could see it all coming together. I looked good. Business would be good today. Men in buying jumpers to keep out the Derry wind would be easily convinced that they should have a new button-down to match. Women picking up hemmed trousers would buy fresh socks or a new belt fer their men. I was doing well at the shop. It was January 1972, that meant the 1971 Salesman of the Year would be awarded soon and I was in the running. I was a good-looking, well-dressed, successful man.

When John Young pinched a school diary from his sister Maura and used it to record his thoughts about girls in town, he had no idea it would become part of his legacy. According to John's diary, girls appeared wherever he went. The fact his closest mates played in a band may have contributed to this phenomenon isn't revealed in his notes and the ticks next to the list of girls at the back of the stolen school diary remain unexplained as well. John seemed to be developing a reputation among his friends for two-timing, but their discord may have stemmed from the fact that John's girlfriend in England was a Protestant. John's attitude was simple: she liked him, what did he care what church she went to?

> Protestant or Catholic didn't bother me, but I was to be eighteen in May and that's just when life begins. I want to enjoy life, not settle down and have a family. I want to move up at the shop, buy a car, make a name for meself. As me mammy always says, 'If you have a job, the world is your oyster.' A final look in the mirror – the hair – perfect.

John had been offered a promotion: a training position in England. He planned to take it. He'd confided in Maura but telling his mother would be a different story. In 1972 Derry was very much a small town. People told their business and weren't reticent in voicing an opinion even in the queue at the shop, 'Don't waste your money on that, I bought one last week and it fell apart.' Except to find work when none was to be had, people stayed in Derry generation on generation. Men went to England and Scotland to find work. They didn't go for promotions.

John's father, Tommy worked for the same company forty-eight years and never received a bonus, promotion, or recognition for a job well done. John's generation was the first generation of Catholic Derry men to find meaningful, rewarding work. They were the first Catholic Derry men to have the opportunity to pursue higher education. John had no intention of being left behind. But John was his mother's son and Derry mothers don't sit well with anyone taking away their sons – even for better jobs and opportunities – so John was putting off telling his mother until it was absolutely necessary.

John Young came from hard-working parents. For ten years, Tommy and Lily walked six miles a day, from Springtown to the city centre and back, for work. His parents set a good example for their children and, like his siblings, John not only enjoyed his work but took it seriously. Jobs and money were hard to come by in Derry, and John understood the power and freedom they offered.

John Temple's was one floor, but upscale. Derry was filled with shirt factories but the shirts in Temple's were imported from England. They carried off-the-rack attire but encouraged special order. John was always well dressed, and he understood the importance of having a suit made to fit. John didn't set out to be a clothier – the headmaster at St Joe's told him about the opening – but there was no better job for him. John's father Tommy was a seed man. His brother Leo was a coal man. John was a clothes man and that suited him.

I hadn't been at work long that Saturday when me ma come in the door. Gosh she was smiling. 'John, you got out the door before I got a chance te see you in your new suit. Let me look at you. You look so handsome.' Then she touched me face. She just looked at me and touched me face – in front of everyone at the shop. Nobody moved. People stared. It started te get uncomfortable. I looked down at her and smiled. 'Go on now Lily. I'll see you at dinner.'

> Imagine me mammy turning up at work like that! What was she thinking? It wouldn't be like her to turn up like that. She worked off Butcher Street on Magazine, just across the Diamond and around the corner, but she didn't turn up at me job, just like I wouldn'ta turned up at hers.

It seemed an odd occurrence at the time, but nobody knew John would be murdered the next day. John's mother, through this act, was granted the gift of remembering her son – tall, handsome, smiling, alive – her John. Until now, most people have known two things about John Young: that he is one of the fourteen murdered by British Paratroopers on Bloody Sunday; and the lies the British Government has told about him. You'd think John was an important person for the British to go to so much trouble to smear his name. The truth is John was just a seventeen-year-old lad who went to a peace march to have a bit of craic with his friends. John wasn't carrying a weapon or throwing a nail-bomb. He pegged a couple of stones but when they turned on the water cannon his vanity about his clothes and hair drove him out.

It's been more than thirty years since John was murdered. He would be fifty this year (29 May 2004) if he'd lived. The stalwart dedication of the families of the killed and wounded in an effort to clear their names has produced two major motion films and a dozen books detailing witness statements and evidence that clearly demonstrate all the victims were unarmed and innocent of any serious wrong-doing on Bloody Sunday. The Bloody Sunday Inquiry, begun in 1998, brought the startling barefaced lies of the soldiers into the public domain. Nonetheless, many people still accept, rather than question, what the British Government told them: that the men and women murdered and wounded on Bloody Sunday got what they deserved; that John Young was a criminal – a Derry Young Hooligan.

It is difficult for people to believe the government would tell outright lies. Jokes about politicians' honesty aside, when the government makes a judgment, people want to believe it is true, or at least partially true. After all, if John were innocent, you or your son might be murdered on any given Sunday. It's not easy to believe the British Government would sanction and then lie about cold-blooded murder in the streets, but that's what they did. So why did they murder John? It would give his family a world of peace to know the answer to that.

Bloody Sunday not only ended and destroyed the lives of twenty-eight men and women, it scarred an entire city. Visit the Bogside today and ask about Bloody Sunday – you'll find the horror and pain are still palpable, but it is likely that the person you talk to will graciously show you the sites, tell you what they witnessed, and hope you will share what you learned.

In 1972 crisis counselling was not available for the 20,000 people who ran for their lives, and the families were told that their sons, daughters, husbands, wives, and parents were responsible for their own deaths and injuries. These innocent civilians were painted as terrorists by a propaganda machine so strong it reached around the world before the final body was delivered to the morgue. John Young was one of twenty-eight killed and wounded by British soldiers on Bloody Sunday. This is his story.

On Christmas Eve, 1948, the Young family arrived at Springtown Camp. They moved in with one chair and twins on the way. Derry's housing shortage goes back long before John was born. Like many places around the world, suffrage was not universal in Northern Ireland. The rule was not one person, one vote but one house, one vote. Therefore, ten adults could be living in the same house but only one vote. The population in Derry was such that gerrymandering was the only way to keep Nationalists under control. This resulted in two typical governmental activities: first, they didn't build houses and second, the few that they did, they crammed into one area so the Catholic population would occupy the fewest constituencies. So, even though a few anti-Unionist candidates managed to get elected to Parliament, their ability to effect substantive change was limited.

For such political reasons people had moved from the Bogside to Springtown Camp. John's mammy, Lily, moved her family to Springtown for smaller reasons. 'Smaller' meaning she was living with another family in a two-bedroom house. Lily was living in a 10 x 10 room with a bed, a fireplace, no running water, outside toilet, a husband and two boys, Patrick and Leo. When she discovered she was pregnant with their third and fourth child, she took action. John's father, Tommy, wasn't crazy about moving three miles out of town, but Lily was determined. Moving with one chair on Christmas Eve, Lily received the best Christmas gift a mother could get – a home of her own.

The U.S. Army Base, Springtown Camp, was a promised land of corrugated tin huts awaiting the cramped Catholic families of Derry. As soon as the Americans left, those living three, four, and five families to a house began a steady migration down the Strand, up Buncrana Road, and out to the huts in Springtown. The abandoned U.S. Army Base was the first taste of freedom for hundreds of Derry families and contributed its own chemistry to the catalyst of the Derry civil-rights movement to come.

When the Young family first moved to Springtown, they had a hut without water. Leo fetched water from the community well. Lily soon discovered the officers' huts and the family moved again. She was thrilled. Lily's home was three bedrooms, living room, indoor toilet, and kitchen. She was ready for the twins. To Lily's heartbreak, one of her babies was stillborn and the other lived just six weeks. Grateful for her job, she returned to the shirt factory and worked away her sorrow.

Life continued at a practical pace for the Young family. Leo walked across the field everyday, taking his shoes and socks off to wade through the stream that cut through Springtown on his way to school. Lily didn't discourage the practice. At least his feet got washed

everyday. When Maura came along and grew big enough to go to school, Leo carried her across the stream – not because he was benevolent – but because she insisted.

Tommy worked for Thompson's Seed Shop. He was lucky to have a job. Few Catholic Derry men were able to find steady work. Tommy's duties included stocking and mixing seed and servicing farm implements. Every day, Monday through to Friday, Tommy rose at five to walk the three miles to work. There were no buses from Springtown and when putting bread on the table and keeping children in shoes was a challenge, a car was a luxury few Catholic families could afford. Lily was happy in her corrugated tin hut so Tommy faithfully completed the journey each day.

Tommy started working in the back of the store hauling and stocking seed when he was fourteen. He wore dungarees and a flat cap. His brother, John, worked at the front of the store and wore a suit. Neither was ever promoted. They worked at the jobs for which they had been hired, and that was that. If a Protestant came to work at the shop, he would be given a better position and better pay than Tommy or John who never earned more than £8 a week. Tommy took retirement at sixty-two because he had developed chronic asthma from the seed dust. His full retirement pay for forty-eight years of work was £360.

A man called Senator Barnhill was the managing director of the store and a Unionist member of the establishment. At 6'3" Senator Barnhill was a big stocky man. He covered his bald head with a wide-brimmed hat, wore a perpetual grin, and travelled on the public bus. Given that he was murdered in 1971 by the Official IRA, he probably wasn't fooling anyone.

Tommy never bothered with politics. He was employed. He had to earn money to put dinner on the table and clothes on his children. There were so few jobs for men in Derry at the time that you took what you could get and didn't complain. Working for Senator Barnhill must have been miserable, though, because for a while everyone in the house suffered, even the dog. The dog would know on the Friday night when Tommy was different, because he would say to the dog during the week, 'Up and we'll go for a walk'. But on a Friday night no walk. The silent treatment. Tommy would take a drink on a Friday, and he'd brood until Sunday noon. Then he'd gather his children and the dog and walk through the oak trees and hawthorn bushes down to the Springtown Bridge and watch the train travelling from Derry to Buncrana.

Lily worked first in Wilkinson's and then Graham Hunter's shirt factories. For about one hundred years, 1874-1974, some of the best shirts in the world came from Derry and these factories employed the women who wanted jobs, which, at 20,000 workers, meant nearly all of them. Lily could sew a shirt from start to finish and when John got older, she always bought his shirts to match his suits.

Lily loved her work. She, too, walked the six-mile return between Derry and Springtown. She left her children with a neighbour and went to work. She loved going to town everyday, working with the women. On bank holidays the shirt-factory girls would organise buses to Donegal or Portrush for a day's outing, dining, and dancing. The friendships she made at the shirt factories and her love of the work would later sustain her as she grieved her murdered son.

Springtown was hard living. The child mortality rate stood at 42 per cent. Domestic violence was rampant. Leo and his friends would often listen to different huts, when people had been at the drink. As objects smashed against tin walls and alighted through windows, they knew there was trouble inside. The boys hung around to hear the craic, but also silently witnessed murder and attendant lawlessness that was kept quiet and written off as rumour.

The Young's experienced their fair share of hardship at Springtown as well. They had more space and a sink with running water, but there was no electricity or heat. There was no washing-up tub and when Leo was older and came home from delivering coal he stood in his underpants as his mother dumped a bucket of water over him and scrubbed him down. The cold of that experience is not something one ever forgets – but that wasn't the only cold. Leo used to say, 'Ye put more clothes on ye going to bed than what ye did when ye're up.' Tommy's mood at the weekend was damaging and hurt Lily more than she could express.

Springtown was hard, but before long joy would come into the house – on 29 May 1954 John was born: 10 pounds, 11 ounces, and the apple of his mammy's eye. From that day, things would be better.

> The only thing I remember about Springtown wasn't about the camp but bein' in hospital for appendicitis. I was a wee wain of three and a half and I remember me mammy hidin' and peeking through the winda. Helen would be sittin' wit me and I'd say, 'There's me ma – I can see the feather in her hat.' She always wore a hat and pearls. She was a very refined, respectable woman and I slagged her, but I loved her more than anything.

Two years later the Young family was allotted a house in Creggan Estates. John and Maura discovered electricity at 120 Westway. With a button at each end, they ran up and down the stairs switching the lights on and off. John's was the back room at the top of the stairs, the smallest room in the house, just big enough for his bed, wardrobe, chest of drawers, and for a while, his father. Patrick and his wife moved into the house so Tommy bunked in with John, and Lily with Maura. With a lino floor and no heat upstairs they still 'put more clothes on ye going to bed than what ye did when ye're up,' so at the least, Tommy added extra warmth to the room for a while.

John had the job of cutting the wee patch of grass and was always sent out to be cutting when a new baby came into the world. In 1963, with three children in tow, Patrick and his wife moved to Shantallow and John finally had his own room – a treasured, guarded possession of the Catholic Derry child.

> Up in Creggan, Maura and I also discovered that Patrick and Leo weren't our only siblings. We had two older sisters as well. Elish and Helen lived at 28 North Street with me mammy's two aunts because there was no room at 32 North for them. Helen and Elish woulda had to walk too far to get to school from Springtown and, they had a choice, so they stayed on in Rosemount wit the two aunts. When Maura was born Helen got taken out of school to help her mammy but Maura and I never knew she was the sister. Maura was thrilled. Didn't make no matter to me. S'long as I got me own room, what did I care how many sisters there were.

Tommy cleaned his shoes every night. He said they kept longer that way. On Saturday nights he took on the boys' shoes as well. He lined them up by the door for the boys to slip on as they left for Mass. John's family gave him endless grief about his feet and shoes. His dad used to say, 'Take a look at them shoes, take a good look at them shoes …' John's response was, 'They're not looking at the shoes, they're looking at me face. This is what they're looking at, from here up.'

> I dunno why I walked the soles off my shoes, they just come off. I once walked to a dance and me feet was bloody from the condition of me shoes. I danced the night away. Did me family take pity on me? No, they give me grief. Me feet were me own business. Maura would say I was a dirty bugger where my feet were concerned, but what was she doin looking at my feet? She said I'd buy three suits for one pair of shoes – but why have two? They'd both be black and nobody would know they were different. If I wore the same suit everyday, the girls would definitely notice, but nobody ever said – is that the same pair of black shoes you wore yesterday?

The time to buy new shoes in Derry would have been right before or after retreat. With all the walking done during that week, you were either buying a pair to break-in or something to replace what you ruined with all the walking. The May retreat meant that for a week you had to be at 6 a.m. Mass, then home for breakfast, down the town to work, home for dinner, back to work, home for tea, and back to chapel from seven till nine. Derry women said they did two weeks retreat every year, for having to get the men up and see that they went.

> At the end of the retreat all of the men wear suits with flowers. You hold onte your flower and give it to your special girlfriend … the number one. Sometimes you give it to just the right girl – but that's probably only if you're engaged or married. 'Cause if you're single, like me, there's always someone gonna be upset.

John was well liked in school by his peers and teachers alike. A good student academically, school also provided the essential social training necessary for later in life. In the midst of John's secondary schooling, a distraught Lily approached Helen:

'I don't know what to do … this will kill your father.'

'Mammy what is it?'

'Oh it's terrible. I didn't raise my son to do this to me.'

'Mother, what's the matter?'

'Our John has dirty books upstairs.'

'Are you sure?'

'Aye.'

'Well, let me see the book.'

'Let you see it?'

'It's alright Mammy I'm married, I have a family – let me see the book.'

'I don't know what the world's coming to …'

Lily showed Helen the book. It was John's biology textbook. Lily replied, 'A school book! Are you kidding? I'll be down to that head-master in the morning!' Lily was forty-three years old when John was born and by the time he reached secondary school her hair was white. Just as the family gave John grief about his feet, he slagged his mother about her white hair, 'Now Ma don't you be coming to school. They'll think you're my granny 'cause you have white hair.'

Ach, she acted sore about that, but she could never be mad at me. I was her John. If she was talking about Helen or Maura, it was 'our Helen, our Maura' but if she was talking about me, it was always, 'my John.'

We was like that, just like any family I s'pose, we'd get mad and huff off, but never for long, and in my case, never far. Once when I was younger, Helen was watching me and (she says) I said something sarcastic so she thumped me. So I said, 'I'm leavin' this house!' But then I had a realisation and changed my mind – 'You don't live here. You go.' Helen stood her ground and told me, 'I'm not goin' – you can go.' So I got me school bag and left. I sat across from the house in the green so she could think about what she done and how much she would miss me. I sat for a long time. Well, least till I got hungry for me dinner.

If John had a falling out with his mother, instead of grounding him, she'd hide his record player. He always found it and then put it back where she had it hidden. She thought she was winning. John spent his money on suits and records. Like just about every other Catholic family in Derry at that time, they didn't have money for anything extra. John quickly learned the power of money and from an early age devised ways of getting it. He worked for it and schemed for it, but he got it nonetheless. One way he worked for his money was by helping the coal delivery man.

> I helped collect the coal money, for one. I could walk inte forty houses in Creggan. Open the door, walk in, lift the coal money, and walk out again. And everybody would say, 'God who was that came in?' and someone in the house would say, 'It's probably just John Young liftin' the coal money.' I used to collect one side of the street, and the man who owned the coal lorry would lift the other. I learnt which houses the pretty girls lived in, and I'd be like, 'Rest yer feet, I'll get this street.'

John had a biscuit tin all felted on the inside. On the outside he wrote 'Save John Young Fund' and when Patrick, Helen, and Leo were up on Sunday, John brought out the box and fined them a shilling for every bad word. Helen was his best customer. He loved to see her coming. She was a guaranteed jackpot. When Helen came in he'd just set the box on her knee.

> Me mammy used to say, 'Food on yer table, clothes on yer back, and ye're grand.' But I wanted more. The money in that box was gonna save me – it was money for me car. I got the job, got the suits, got the girls, my next conquest – the car.

John managed to save some money but there were important expenses he had to keep up with like suits, records, and girls. So he took advantage of every opportunity. Helen supplied the record player and chess board – gifts to her favourite brother. John 'roadied' for Roddy's band and got in free to all the dances they played. Lily got a discount at the shirt factory so she bought the shirts for his suits. 'See, everything worked out. How could it not? I was me. John Young. Life was good.'

Every Thursday and Saturday me and Maura would go down to Helen's to watch the colour TV. Me and Helen was trekkies and didn't miss a Thursday night. But Saturday's Helen would sometimes be out on her civil-rights marches and then I hadda watch what Maura picked. Don't know why exactly Helen kept goin' to them marches. She started goin' 'cause she wanted a house to get outta that 10 x 10 back room she and her husband and three girls were livin' in. Anyway, she'd got a house and she had a colour TV, so why she was out still marchin' and not home relaxin' was beyond me.

Maura and John never expressed any interest in the marches. They had it good. They lived in a big house with their own rooms. They had jobs and therefore some disposable income. They had not experienced sectarian violence and generally lived quiet, happy teenage lives. They also worked on Saturdays when the marches were held.

I could see them marchers going right past the shop. Out marchin' in the rain and the cold. That didn't appeal to me. Gettin' off with the girls, makin' money, going to England, gettin' a car. I had my priorities.

On 30 January 1972 the first Sunday Derry civil-rights march was held. Many people worked on a Saturday, but Sunday was a day of rest and relaxation – you went to Mass, cooked your dinner, visited with family and friends. Therefore, this particular march drew whole families and groups of friends, many of whom had never attended a civil-rights march. Patrick, Leo, Helen, Maura, and John all departed from 120 Westway. Helen and Patrick went to support civil rights; John and Maura went for the craic; Leo went along to keep after John.

How could I miss this march? Every girl in Derry and a whole lot from Belfast were out. I wore my grey trousers, striped shirt, grey jumper, the bomber jacket that my number one Derry girl ordered from America, and a hat. It was dry but I'd be out all the afternoon and I didn't like it rainin' on me and messin' up me hair. Me friend Joe slagged me bout dressin' up for a march – but I knew he'd regret not looking good. Most of the girls I seen were still in their Sunday dresses. The craic was good. It would be a good day.

It turned out to be a tragic day. John became a well-dressed corpse, an incidental martyr whom the government and public press degraded and ridiculed. John Young was well named – too young to die and too innocent to be defamed. John's grave stands quietly in the city cemetery. But he is not at rest. John's presence is strong in Derry, and thirty-one years later the people who loved him continue to walk the soles off their shoes to clear his name, so some day he may truly rest in peace.

Hugh Gilmour

If mischief were around, it would find Hugh Gilmour.

Hugh was the baby of the house. The youngest of nine, small and wiry, his family called him the German, in honour of his flat head. Keeping track of Hugh was no easy task and two brothers, Bernard and Floyd, were assigned to look after him. Every day Bernard and Floyd were sent – 'Get Hugh. Bring Hugh in. Go see where Hugh is. If he's in a safe place, well, that's OK, stay there.'

Hugh Gilmour was born at 16 Springtown Camp in 1954. The entire Gilmour family lived together in Springtown. The four girls, Olive, Doreen, Sara, and Brigid in one bedroom; the boys, Tony, Bernard, and Floyd in the other – packed like sardines. Hugh, being the baby, stayed with his parents Henry and Kathleen. 'They must a thought we'd smother him, or choke him, or maybe we'da been that hungry sometimes we'd probably eat him,' said Bernard, 'Keep him away, they'll probably eat him.'

Hugh was perhaps the nuttiest member of his family, but being the youngest earned him a coveted place in the household pecking order. According to his brothers and sisters, Hugh's position meant he got more than they ever did. Not that the family had much but, while his seven brothers and sisters went to school without shoes, Hugh always had them. While the rest of the siblings regularly beat the hell out of each other, nobody was allowed to touch Hugh. He wasn't to be hit. 'He's too small.' If the brothers touched the German, his mother and sisters rallied to his defense.

Fortunately enough, it never became an issue. Hugh was his mother's world and his mother was Hugh's. One of his great loves in life. The other children were sensible enough to watch themselves. The German went head-long into anything. So Kathleen employed them, Olive, Tony, Doreen, Bernard, Floyd, Sarah, and Brigid, one after the other to watch after Hugh. Bernard and Floyd, on German-patrol before leaving for Scotland, were sent in to respond to a letter from the primary school headmaster that Hugh was not attending all his classes. Their orders were to 'take him over to school, and into the classroom, and make sure he goes to class.' Bernard and Floyd went to the headmaster who said, 'Hugh's not here, he doesn't come to school here.'

'Aye, he does.'

'No, Hugh comes in here for his dinner, and goes back out again.'

'Would ye not keep him in?'

'Stay there and watch – watch for Hugh coming in. He'll be in at noon.'

Bernard and Floyd watched and waited. They didn't see Hugh come in.

'Well I don't know what happened today, I see him every other day.'

Hugh was smart, he knew Bernard and Floyd were there. He had managed to evade his captors. Bernard and Floyd left the front door and went down to the canteen and sure enough, there was the German, eating his dinner. Bernard and Floyd stood guard in the corridor to escort Hugh to class. His class came through, but no Hugh. The German had escaped over the roof of the canteen with the help of a builder's scaffolding. Later at home, Bernard led the interrogation:

'We were in your school today.'

'Aye I seen ye.'

'Where did ye go?'

'I went inte me class.'

'Ye jumped over the roof and down.'

'Aye, I was down sittin' wi' big Gerry the caretaker.'

'Naw ye weren't, ye sneaked off and ye went somewhere else.'

Reconnaissance and interrogation complete, Bernard and Floyd went back to the headmaster who said, 'He does that every day, he comes in here for his lunch and goes again, that's the only reason I wrote a letter to your mother, to make sure he doesn't get into bother.'

'Why ye not stop him?'

'You try and stop him. If you can get over the roof as quick as that wee boy there … there he is now. Look! Try and stop him.'

'I will, aye.'

Hugh was up the top of the scaffold and back down again, like a monkey. All muscle and mischief, there was no stopping Hugh Gilmour. He enjoyed his school dinner unencumbered from then on.

Hugh's brothers left home to find work at early ages. By the time Hugh reached the proper beatin'-up age or had enough meat on him to make a decent meal, Tony, the eldest son, left home. He went to England at sixteen and joined the Royal Air Force. As soon as Bernard and Floyd were relieved of duty − patrolling the streets for the German − they went to pick spuds in Scotland. Unfortunately, finding Hugh would take on tragic significance before any member of the family was prepared for it.

The family moved from Springtown in 1960 to a small street in the Bogside called Pilot's Row, Hugh lost no time making friends. These friendships were forged by freedom and geography. As soon as all of his six-year-old self stepped out the front door, Hugh's closest friends became Gerry Doherty, Jim Duffy, Jack McDonald, and Andy McCauley. Hugh was christened 'Gilly', and although fate would intervene from time to time, the bond of these friends was unbreakable for the next ten years.

If ever there were a gaggle of ruffians roaming the streets, it was Hugh and his friends. Closed on Sunday, the docks provided plenty of opportunity for exploring and futtering about. The day might start with a walk from the top of the docks to the bottom. A bakery, called Hunters, dumped the days' unused dough and pastry, which the boys collected for feasting and fishing up the docks. Along the way the boys took turns, 'What if you went down here in the river and found a dead body …' as they walked two miles back to the slaughter houses where pig entrails were flushed into the river.

Present at the right time, the moment of the flush, you could catch a mullet – the rat of the sea. Mullets would eat anything, and they feasted on pig entrails. With string lifted from building sites, the boys constructed lines, attached dough, and bobbed it on the surface of the water. When the mullet took the dough and went down, they hooked it, reeled it in, and chopped it up to use for bait to fish for flukes and eel.

Walking two miles looking for a piece of dough with which to catch a mullet that would then be cut up and used to fish for flukes made perfect sense to the boys because you could eat a fluke, a flat fish like a plaice. Once you knew what a mullet ate, nobody could eat it, but you could eat the flukes so that was the goal. Not that they were crack fishermen. There was an old crane at that part of the river, and the boys spent more time swinging on its hook than they did fishing. So they weren't great fishermen, but they liked to think that they were.

In spite of their antics, Hugh and his friends were gentlemen. They pulled a lot of stunts among each other but remained polite and respectful to their elders. When it was time for Hugh to come in for his dinner or bed, his father whistled – a sharp twittering whistle. Hugh would whistle back and home he'd go quick as a flash. He would never utter a bad word to his parents.

The boys often spent an evening listening to the yarns of an old night watchman who sat in a hut like a sentry box with a brazier full of coke, the cheapest form of heating fuel. The 'old' watchman was forty years old or so, but the boys thought he was ancient. So they gathered around the hut, erected for the watchman to guard a hole in the road or some other pressing duty surrounded by the sulphurous smoke of the coke, listening to yarns of the man's exploits about England and other exotic destinations. The boys pumped away at him, 'Go on tell us again about …' and he spun yarns long into the evening just to keep them there and help kill the time. The boys listened intently – any excuse to stay out another moment longer – hoping their parents would forget the time. But true to form, Hugh's dad sent out the timely call. The sharp-twittering whistle piercing the night air sent the boys home to get a clip on the ear for smelling of sulphur.

A five-man Derry clean-up crew, the boys would do anything to earn a couple of shillings. They would plunder old derelict houses looking for lead, copper wire, scrap iron, and wood, anything that could be turned into money. During one of these forays they uncovered a German life-raft complete with insignia. They had visions of floating down the river, but when they tried to blow it up it was full of holes. They'd sell what they could to the scrap man for a couple of shillings which they turned over for sweets or saved until they had enough for a day's hire of bikes to ride to the seaside at Buncrana.

In another scheme to earn money, the boys collected old wood from houses set for demolition and unused wooden pallets from all over town. They sat in the backyard and broke and chopped it up and made bundles of sticks to sell. They were always on the hunt for bits of elastic to bind the bundles. Cutting up old bicycle tubes was one solution and on this particular day, Hugh lifted some tubes hanging in his father's shed – 'These old things'll work, right?' Hugh's father came in that evening and said to Bernard, 'I was going te ride down te Buncrana, but somebody's stole me tyres. Broke inte the wee shed down there and cut me tyres up and off the bike.' Hugh sat staring sideways at Bernard, sheepish grin affixed to his face, nodding.

Summertime was the go-carting season, a time when everyone in the district made a go-cart to race down the Derry walls. A go-cart at that time was a complicated piece of machinery for a ten-year-old to construct. First, they had to find the wheels: large ones for the back; small ones for the front. These were found by knocking on doors and asking for old prams. Then the body had to be constructed out of wood. The boys had no access to drills so the hole attaching the front axle had to be burned through the wood using a hot poker. This took time and patience – something the boys had in abundance. All this, however, was worthwhile when racing season began. Some guys were better than others at building carts; especially those who had access to paint. This process was repeated in the winter, without wheels of course, during sleigh-making season.

Collecting wood, tyres, and anything that would burn was a year-round activity in preparation for the annual 15 August bonfire. With the fire roaring, they would sit at the end of the street telling ghost stories – trying to scare the pants off each other – seeing who could come up with the best story. Sneaking into the cinema by using a coat hanger to open the fire-exit door and then crawling on hands and knees to find a seat; stealing apples from orchards; and experimenting with smoking by cutting unfiltered fags in half was the extent of the young lads' lawless behaviour. But in 1968, events in Derry would radically change the boys' lives.

'Daring' only began to describe Gilly. One of his more popular stunts was scaling the multi-story flats where he lived. Hugh would place his back against a column which supported the catwalks crossing between each block of flats. The column was two feet from the main wall. From this position Hugh inched his way up from floor to floor, pausing at about ninety feet to brush his hands dramatically and wave to his friends below who were petrified at this spectacle. Gilly also discovered riding inside the lifts was optional. Instead, they could ride on top. Going up required a properly timed dive to disembark without being crushed. When crossing Craigavon Bridge, linking the Cityside and Waterside, a normal person chose the footpath. Not Gilly, he chose to walk on the four-inch parapet of the railings. Coming in covered in dirt and grease at the end of each day his mother would ask, 'What were you up to?' 'Nothin', Ma.'

While swimming in the Faughan River one day, Gilly's friend Andy was pulled under by the current. John Duffy, fishing nearby, went into the river but the boy was caught up on some wire rubbish that had been dumped into the river. Andy could not be brought up in time. Hugh and his mates went silent as church mice. They didn't go home crying. They didn't reveal their secret to their parents. None of the boys spoke a word. Their families found out about the tragedy when the police showed up at their homes to question the boys the next day.

Not telling about the death of his friend was part of Hugh's world. He and his mates did daring stunts all around town, but no one ever told. Admitting that had Andy drowned would have been like tattling. The lads' one true vice was loyalty. They never ratted each other out. They weren't calloused – Hugh and his mates suffered the loss of their friend, it was a sad time for them, their families could see it – but the lads would never tell.

Andy's father had received a commendation for rescuing a sailor who fell from his ship into the River Foyle. It was ironic that at Andy's wake the award his father earned for rescuing a drowning man hung near the coffin of his drowned son. In Andy's death was a helplessness far too many Derry families would experience in the years to come.

On 5 October 1968, Gerry and Hugh went down to the Templemore School football pitch for a game and no one showed up. So they spent an hour running around after frogs – just chasing frogs around the field trying to catch them. Tired of frog-chasing, they wandered down to the bottom of the pitch, which took them out onto the Buncrana Road where they could catch the bus back to town. They headed into town but the bus was diverted up along the back of the quay – which was unusual. The driver took them across the double-decker bridge and dropped them off at HMS *Sea Eagle*, a British Naval Base. They couldn't figure out why the bus hadn't stopped at the Guildhall but instead taken them all the way over to the Waterside. Nonetheless, they didn't ask any questions and just headed back to town. They didn't know there had been a baton charge up Duke Street through a civil-rights march and that people were all beat up.

As they walked home they came across discarded placards, streets hosed with water, police tenders, and cops in riot gear. The hassle they got crossing the bridge into town was hotter than usual but they really didn't think much of it. They were just two kids. Oblivious, Hugh and Gerry crossed the Diamond and turned down Butcher Street to find a full-blown riot – people kicking in windows of shops, stones hurled at the police, and just as they reached the gate, the RUC made another baton charge.

As the boys fled, Hugh down the bank of the flats and Gerry down Faughan Street, Bang! Gerry's head opened up – split open by a rock from one side or the other. He couldn't tell and didn't care which. He just couldn't believe it, an hour before he was chasing frogs in a field and now his head was split open in a riot. And so, at the end of the day, Gerry and Hugh found themselves throwing stones at the police. They didn't know exactly why they were throwing stones or why exactly the police were there; they just did what everybody else was doing.

Sporadic rioting continued throughout the year culminating in the Battle of the Bogside, which took place in August of 1969. During those three days, men occupied the roof of the Rossville Flats as a vantage point. Gerry and Hugh were given the assignment of delivering a box of looted apples to the roof of the flats. Arriving with the apples, Hugh was ready to join the lads preparing petrol bombs. Gerry was not as impressed, 'What the fuck are youse doing up ere? The cops are way down there.'

'Stay up here,' Hugh tells him, ''Cause when they come in, ya got a good shot at the cops.' Gerry sat up there for a while but boredom set in and he was away. Later that day a journalist snapped a photo of Hugh on the roof, at the ready (see opposite page).

After three days and nights of rioting, the British Army was deployed onto the streets forming a buffer zone between the rioters and the police. As a result of that riot and the distrust the police created by their actions over the previous year, the Bogside residents built barricades around their area forming Free Derry. Here the writ of the British Government did not run.

Hugh's family had moved to the flats in 1965. By the end of 1969 the boys began to drift apart. They left school, got work, and developed different interests. Go-cart building and frog catching gave way to girls, jobs, and cars. Although only a few steps away, they lived in different neighbourhoods. They made new friends and fell out of touch. The friendships closed and faded away as fate, geography, and politics intervened. But the memories of a wonderful carefree childhood endured.

Aptly named the Gilly-mobile, one of Hugh's greatest loves in

life was his car. While the origin of the car is unknown, whether someone gave it to him or he paid £20, the fact that it was Hugh's first love was clear. Throughout the last half of 1971, Hugh and his friends, Christy Tucker and Thomas Barr, would put five or six shillings together for petrol, and drive the old Austin 40 all over creation. 'Bern, we're doing 38 mph!' That car wouldn't do 10 mph, and barely reached 30 down a hill. With no brakes in the car, Hugh's friends had to leap out of the car on the way down the hill to stop it.

The lads painted a white stripe along a curb of the car park and lettered 'GILLY'S CAR PARK, LIVERPOOL' in black. That of course is where they always pushed the car – home base. Nobody else was allowed to park there, so Hugh's family always knew when he was out. From their window in the flats they watched the lads racing off in the car and pushing it back again.

Every day, here would come Hugh and the lads, pushing it back to base. Another few shillings, another gallon of petrol, and they were driving all around town. When she ran out of petrol, push her back again. They'd be three miles away from home but they'd still push her all the way. They would never abandon the wee A-40. After Hugh was murdered, his family looked down one day to see the car was burning. A sad sight, because that was his life.

Hugh and his friends continued their turns throwing stones at the RUC and later the British Army. But pretty much everybody in the Bogside took a turn throwing stones or bottles at one time or another. The game with the soldiers was just too enticing for most to resist, including teenagers, mothers, small children, and the elderly. Nobody ever thought some boys would come across the Irish Sea, shoot Gilly, then go back to their barracks and congratulate each other.

Hugh wasn't an IRA man or a terrorist. He was a wee lad of seventeen. His mother scrubbed his back for him at the end of the day. Hugh would come in from his work as a tyre fitter, stand at the sink, and she would wash his back, 'scratch me back now Mammy, down another wee bit, aye wash there Mammy' but as soon as somebody came in, he was embarrassed. If Bernard came in and said, 'Are ye washin' him again?' The German replied, 'She is not, shutup!'

Hugh was his mother's son. She didn't sleep until he was in at night. She sent Bernard or Floyd after him if it were past eleven. Hugh rested his head on her knee as they talked. She went to his room and watched him sleep. Hugh and his mother shared a deep and abiding love for one another. Hugh was a Derry mother's son.

One day at work a big tyre fell and broke his toes. He wouldn't go to hospital. He walked to work with the foot inside his mother's slipper. He walked to work in the house shoe and put his boot on when he got to work. Even though he was a mammy's boy, Hugh wasn't the type to ask for help. His mother would say, 'Go on and help him up.' 'Naw I'm alright. I'm grand.'

He climbed trees, stole apples out of orchards, drove his car around with friends ready to employ the brakes, smoke flying out of the end of it, lads coughing up shillings for the petrol. They threw stones at the army, rode the top of the lifts, walked the railings, plenty of things – crazy, but nothing bad. Hugh and his friends had respect for their elders, they saluted the priest in the street, kept their misfortune quiet, took their oil, and kept their friends' secrets. Hugh was mischievous, 'Bern, we're doing 38 mph!' and oh, that smile – that was Gilly – Hugh Gilmour, man about town.

On 30 January 1972 another civil-rights march took place. Since the first Derry march on 5 October 1968, the peace march had been a powerful way to attract media attention to civil-rights issues in Northern Ireland. Some were peaceful, some ended in riots and injury. Still, none of the 20,000 marchers on this Sunday expected murder and mayhem.

Before he left for the march, Hugh gave his mother a half crown for her birthday. He said to her, 'That's fer yer birthday.' He wasn't a boy given to much hugging. He kissed her and said, 'There, that's all ye're gettin.' And away he went.

In 1972, the British Army stated that Free Derry was an IRA haven. The reality was the Derry IRA was a small force seriously out-manned and out-gunned by the British Army. Derry men were drawn in by the peaceful-protest scheme and while they marched in protest, threw stones at the army, and eventually shut down the Bogside to British incursion, they were not queuing up to join the IRA.

Even so, somehow those army boys coming over got it into their heads there was some force to fear and on 30 January 1972, they murdered unarmed civil-rights demonstrators in the streets. If Hugh had joined the IRA and been shot, his family would have been devastated, but they would have been proud of him for fighting for his people. That wasn't the reality. Hugh was a civilian murdered in the street, and from that his family never fully recovered. The Paras shot Hugh as he and others fled for their lives and then went back to their barracks to celebrate.

That Sunday evening Bernard was sent out for the last time to find the German. Everybody thought Hugh was wounded. At Altnagelvin Hospital Bernard said to a couple of boys, 'Did ye see Hugh?' 'He's over there. He's wounded. Been shot in the arm.' Sorting through the wounded in wards eight and nine, Bernard and Olive were unable to find Hugh. Rumours circulated that some of the wounded had been taken to Letterkenny but these turned out to be false hopes of people desperate to find sons, brothers, and husbands alive. Bernard and Olive made their way to the morgue, identified Hugh, and went home to face their mother.

They went home with the news, 'Hugh's not wounded. He's dead.' Kathleen sat in denial until Hugh's body was brought home. His beautiful face at peace, his appearance neat and tidy in his coffin belied his last moments of pandemonium and terror: people screaming, bullets flying, CS gas in the air, being advanced upon by black-faced soldiers trained to kill, lying in the arms of young marcher Geraldine Richmond crying, 'Mammy! Get me Mammy!'

After the funeral, after Hugh's coffin was lowered into the ground; after the cold sound of dirt hitting wood faded away, his family was left with a gaping wound. Gilly had been murdered. There was no more searching for the missing German; no more jokes; no more games. There was no back to scrub; hair to tussle; not one darling boy to watch while he slept. Nothing to do but pass his room; go up to his bed; look at his clothes hanging in the closet still holding his form, waiting to be pulled out for another day at Northern Ireland Tyre. No broken toes to fill a slipper. No mischievous grin. No one left to push the wee A-40 into Gilly's Car Park. Kathleen would never again receive a half crown for her birthday or a wink and a smile.

'I wonder why they shot Hugh?' Kathleen asked. 'Why not shoot the man in front of him or beside him? Why him? There were thousands there – how'd they happen to pick him out? What was that boy thinking when he shot Hugh? Ah – he probably feels bad fer it now, ye know.'

'Why did it kill him?' Bernard wondered. 'Why didn't the bullet just pass though him and wound him? He'd a wile bad run when ye think o' it – it was bad luck that they shot him, and worse luck that he died from it, ye know.'

Bernard, no more than twenty yards away, couldn't hear his brother crying for his mother. He didn't know that Hugh was dying. 'Mammy, go an' get me Mammy.' They were just around the corner. They could see his feet. They didn't know he was dying. From her window Kathleen could see him but she didn't know it was him. She could see his feet on the ground, but she didn't know it was Hugh. The image plagued her – how could she not know? Isn't a mother supposed to know? Isn't a mother supposed to hear when her child is crying out to her?

After Hugh's death, Kathleen was annoyed she had so few photographs of him. First Holy Communion, Confirmation, retreats, friends, she had only memories, no photos. It wasn't unusual. When you're happy to have bread and your children go without shoes, a camera isn't at the top of your wish list. Besides, a mother doesn't record things so she can remember them in the event of her son's death. Mothers die before their sons. That's the proper course of life.

Kathleen loved talking about Hugh up to the day she died. If anyone else talked about Hugh, she loved it. But the television footage haunted Kathleen. There were the Paras entering the Bogside, 'Hugh's still alive. There, look, in the crowd, is that Hugh there?' Bernard would respond, 'Naw that's not him. Naw, he's away down in the flats somewhere.' But whenever that bit of the footage was played she insisted. 'Hugh's still alive there, look.'

Hugh's family desperately wanted to stop time. If they could just step into that moment, go into the picture, and move Hugh from that place. If Bernard could just move time back twenty seconds when Hugh ran past him at the door, he could shout at him to come in. All Hugh needed to hear was his father's sharp twittering whistle and quick as a flash, he'd be home.

Gerald Donaghey

Three devastating losses. One remarkable woman.

Mary Donaghey's life has not been easy. She buried her father, mother, and brother. If burying three family members wasn't enough, of all the Bloody Sunday families she's had the toughest job clearing her brother's name. So difficult that she was initially kept at arm's length by other families because they believed Gerald's case tainted the others. Gerald was no angel. Firstly, he was a teenage boy. Teenage boys, even the good ones, are rarely described as angels. Gerald was a member of Fianna Eireann. His buddy Gearóid O'hEara was the leader of that pack. Gerald avoided jail for a time and went on 'holiday' in the Free State. He probably pegged stones at soldiers. He was no angel. Few in Derry, whether Protestant, Catholic, government, or civilian were saintly in 1972. That doesn't make him guilty of carrying nail bombs on Bloody Sunday.

Nail bombs are awkward buggers. Constructing one is not a difficult task but it is messy and it is impossible to build one without getting gelignite all over your hands and the bomb itself. Therefore, even if he didn't build the bombs, his hands, jeans, and jacket would have been contaminated when he shoved the bombs in his pockets. The tests for explosives residue on Gerald's hands were inconclusive as 'Dr Martin did not regard the results of the tests on Donaghey as positive but Professor Simpson did.'[25]

The recipe for a nail bomb is fairly simple:

1. Gelignite – four to six inches per bomb
2. Corrugated cardboard

3. Nails – preferably the 16-penny size
4. Fuse – typically in 5-6 second lengths
5. Detonators
6. Electrical Tape
7. Red-tipped Matches

Cut the gelignite into the desired length. Slide the nails in alter-
nating directions into the cardboard. Wrap the nail-lined cardboard
around the gelignite. Secure with tape (wrap completely, leaving
top exposed). Make a small hole or well in the top of the gelignite
about half-way down the interior. Place one end of the fuse inside
the detonator and crimp detonator to secure fuse. Cut fuse at a 45
degree angle to expose gunpowder. Tape several matches to the end
of the fuse. Put fuse, detonator-end first, into the well. Secure fuse
with tape. If you can do all that without contaminating yourself, the
bomb, and everything around you – you are a better bomb-builder
than I am. Finally, try shoving the thing in jeans you wore in the
'70s and running down the street. Good luck.

Gerald was shot by Soldier G as he fled from the soldiers' opening
fire in Rossville Flats. The crowd ran across Rossville Street, along
the south end of Glenfada Park North, between the buildings and
into Abbey Park. Soldiers firing and people falling all along the way.
By the time Gerald went down, bodies had dropped all around him
– Patrick O'Donnell, Joseph Mahon, Joseph Friel, Michael Quinn,
and Danny Gillespie lay wounded. Jim Wray, William McKinney, and
Gerald McKinney were dead or dying. In fact, the bullet that blew
the five centimetre hole in his stomach, may have passed through
Gerry McKinney before hitting Gerald.

There are too many unanswered questions to convict Gerald
Donaghey of carrying nail bombs on Bloody Sunday. The first point
that confounds is the nail-bombs don't turn up in anyone's testimony
until he arrives at Coy HQ. Denis McFeely, Raymond Rogan, Mrs
Rogan, Leo Young, and Dr Swords tended Gerald at the scene. None
of them saw nail-bombs and Denis admits if he had seen nail bombs
in Gerald's pockets, he would have removed them himself. Raymond
Rogan brought Gerald into his house where his wife and five children were. He loaded Gerald into his car. Had he no care for the
safety of his family or himself? Leo Young held Gerald in the back

of Rogan's car. Did they just throw caution to the wind and decide to drive to hospital with four nail bombs in the car?

Six soldiers testified they were present when the car was stopped on Barrack Street, that Gerald was examined to determine he was dead and that the car, with Gerald still inside, was then taken to Coy HQ. None of their statements mention nail-bombs. Why didn't they call for an ambulance? Were the soldiers qualified to certify death? Why did they take the car to HQ and not to the hospital or morgue? What was their motive? If Gerald did have nail-bombs shoved in his pockets, wasn't the commanding officer putting his men in danger when he ordered them to drive the car to HQ?

Then there's the testimony of Dr Martin. His notes indicate that the bullet passed through the lower left-front pocket of the jacket, leaving a ragged hole. An apparently undamaged nail bomb had been recovered from this pocket and yet nothing in the notes suggests that Dr Martin considered there was a possible conflict of evidence needing to be resolved.

However, Dr Hall, an explosives expert at DIFS, recalls that he placed the nail bomb taken from the lower left pocket back into that pocket in order to determine whether or not a bullet could have passed through without striking the nail bomb. (BSI Statement Para

48) Dr Hall concluded it could only have occurred if the nail bomb had been placed deep into the pocket, but not if the bomb were half out of the pocket.

These tests do not appear to have been documented nor does it appear that notes were made of any discussions between Dr Martin and Dr Hall on the matter. Neither Dr Martin nor Dr Hall dealt with the issue in their reports or testimony to Widgery. Also, the explosives residue only turned up in two pockets.

Item (1) consisted of a blue-denim jacket. Both side pockets had been recently cut open and a nitrate ester consistent with nitroglycerine was detected on the inside surface of the right pocket. Both breast pockets were intact and, no explosive residues were detected. Item (2) consisted of a blue-woolen sweater. No explosives residues were detected on its surface. Item (3) consisted of a blue shirt. No explosives residues were detected on its surface. Item (4) consisted of a white handkerchief. No explosive residues were detected on its surface. Items (5) and (7) consisted of underclothes and were not examined for explosives. Item (6) consisted of a pair of blue-denim jeans. The left-side pocket had been recently cut open but no explosive residues were detected in any of the other three pockets or on the outside surface. Item (8) consisted of a pair of black leather boots. No explosive residues were detected on their surface.

Nor was any explosives residue found on Gerald's hands. How does a person handle four nail-bombs and not get any explosives residue on him? It is practically impossible – if Gerald did not make the bombs, and even if the bombs sat for months before use, once he picked them up, his hands would have been tainted. How do you shove four nail-bombs in your pockets without touching any of your clothes? He was a boy. He likely wiped his hands on his jacket or shirt. Yet there was no trace of explosives residue.

According to Professor Dermot Walsh:

> Very strong circumstantial evidence suggests that the bombs were not present until just before they were found on him. One of the bombs in his jacket was so tightly squeezed into the pocket that it had to be cut out. Moreover, his jeans were tightly fitted with pockets opening to the front. Any bombs in these pockets would have been clearly visible. Indeed, when the first one was spotted it was actually sticking out of the top of his pocket. Nevertheless, they were not spotted by Dr Swords, who examined him shortly after he was shot. It was worth noting here that Dr Swords actually searched his pockets for identification. They were also not spotted by the army medical officer who examined the body twice, actually opening the front of the trousers in the process. There was also compelling evidence that the position of the body had been moved on the seat after the medical officers' last examination and the time when the bombs were discovered. Finally, there was ample opportunity for the bombs to have been planted after the body had been examined by the medical officer and before the bombs were found. All in all, the case for concluding that the bombs were planted seems more credible than the reverse.[26]

The nature of the entry wound led Dr Swords to believe that if Gerald had been taken immediately to hospital, he could have survived. But he didn't make it to hospital. The car was stopped and taken to the army medical post on Craigavon Bridge (Coy HQ). Entering through the stomach, the bullet lacerated his aorta and inferior vena cava. It passed through his intestines and lodged in his back. Gerald bled to death, five pints of blood slowly leaking into his stomach, as he lay in the back of Raymond Rogan's Cortina.

The pain and loss Gerald's family suffered after his murder have never eased. The lies about Gerald's life, of IRA men, nail-bombs, and conviction, have been told hundreds of times over by the British Government and public press. Mary Donaghey has earned the right to tell her brother's life story: the way she remembers it.

The photo of Gerald as a beautiful blue-eyed, blond curly-haired baby in his blue fur coat and white boots has been lost to the years but the love of the Donaghey family and their memories of a quiet boy who captured his family's heart live on.

Scampering down the red-lino stairs, through the long hall, past the living room, and out to play skipping on the street was one of Gerald's favourite treats. But more often his route was over the red-, black-, blue-, green-, and white-squared lino of the scullery and out the back for games with neighbourhood pals. Keeping her children close to the apron, Rebecca created a children's play paradise of grass free from plantings or flowers.

Whether they came for sweets or games is a closely guarded secret, but as the neighbourhood filled with the aroma of Rebecca's apple cakes, pies, and scones, her backyard swarmed with children. Gerald's father filled the house with music, playing piano and guitar while the children sang along. At the weekend the house was full of adults. Women knitting and chatting and men playing cards were equally happy to find trays filled with cakes and pies.

As soon as Patrick was born, Rebecca left her job at the shirt factory to be home. Rebecca adored her children and thus was not the disciplinarian in the house. Never able to stay cross with them for long, the children were often called from their rooms for a treat. Rebecca preferred talking with her children to thumping them when they got out of order, and sang to them in her sweet soft voice when they were hurt, scared, or sick. Small gifts were left for the children whenever she could arrange them: a pram for Mary's doll, a tin of sweets, a ball for her boys.

Charles showered affection on his children as well and rose every morning to make their breakfast and chat before they left for school or work. On Friday, Charles stopped for a stout at Duffy's on Rossville Street, and then headed home with fish and chips. Patrick,

Mary, and Gerald watched expectantly from the front window for his tall, lean figure to come ambling up the hill. They were frequently discouraged when Charles kept one hand behind his back. Did he have the dinner, or didn't he? Charles enjoyed seeing their distressed faces turn to joy when he produced the hidden treasure.

Family life was sweet for the Donagheys; sometimes too sweet. One afternoon Mary came home from school to a strange but familiar scent. It wafted down the street, getting stronger and stronger as she approached and entered the house. While she'd never smelled it in quite such a concentrated form, it reminded her of Manhattan, the perfume she'd saved for weeks to buy. As she climbed the stairs there at the landing stood the culprit – six-year-old Gerald happily spraying the final contents of the coveted bottle. Mary took out after Gerald but Rebecca intervened, telling Mary she could always get another perfume but this was her brother – and there was no replacement for him. Rebecca didn't hit her children, and she wasn't going to allow them to thump each other.

When Gerald was eight years old, his mother started keeping him home from school from time to time. Rebecca hid Gerald in the wardrobe until Charles left for work. As soon as he was gone, she and Gerald would play games, bake, and sing songs. Rebecca and Gerald enjoyed their stolen time together until the day Charles forgot his lunch. Rebecca and Gerald were busted and their intrigues together came to an immediate end. Perhaps Rebecca sensed something was afoot and just wanted every moment with her son, as Rebecca soon learned she had cancer. A swollen thyroid gland, followed by a lump in the neck, proved to be throat cancer.

Back at school, Gerald worked hard, did his homework, and was considered by his teachers to be a very smart boy. His brother left for seminary to become a priest. Life continued happily for the Donaghey's for the next four years. Family holidays to Buncrana, walks on a Sunday at Hollywell Hill, grand Christmas celebrations, wonderful cakes for birthdays, and always a house filled with friends, songs, and laughter. It was good. And then, it was over.

The Donaghey's happy life would be forever altered in 1965. On 10 December Charles fell while changing a light bulb at the Post Office. Attended by Dr Sullivan Jr, at hospital, Charles was sent home to rest in his bed. Alarmed at his rapidly deteriorating condition, Rebecca phoned Dr Crawdey on Saturday morning who came out and immediately phoned the ambulance. Charles had been bleeding internally. At hospital, Charles implored Mary to care for her mother and brothers. Mary authorised emergency surgery when police arrived with release papers that night.

On Sunday morning Charles sat up in his hospital bed. He said, 'Me Da was in te talk te me the day. He was sitting at the end of me bed this morning.' A bit delirious, Mary thought, but he's up and talking – good news. He fell from his hospital bed that night and on Tuesday 14 December, Charles died.

Rebecca lost all heart longing for her dead husband and followed him just four weeks later on 13 January 1966. Attending seminary in Spain, Patrick didn't receive the news of his father's death until after Charles was buried. When Rebecca's doctor broke the news that Rebecca was also soon to die, someone suggested to Father Daly that he write to the seminary Patrick attended. Fr Daly obliged, and Patrick came home. The cancer in her throat had taken her lovely melodious voice and at the end she motioned for Patrick and Mary to take care of Gerald. Essentially orphaned, the post office took up a negligence case against the hospital on behalf of Patrick, Mary, and Gerald. The case was settled out of court for less than it took to feed the family for a year.

Mary, nineteen years old, confused and devastated over the loss of her parents, refused to let her family be further torn apart. Gerald was scared. He was convinced that without their parents he and his siblings would be separated. He desperately missed his mother – his champion, confidant, and first true love. Patrick returned to Spain and Mary kept what was left of her family intact. A smaller family perhaps, but filled with love and a friendship that would deepen, grow, and blossom.

In the years Mary nurtured him, Gerald grew from a quiet boy into a confident young man. He liked football, music, dancing at the Stardust, and was very congenial. At home he was good-natured and quiet. He and Mary would often spend an evening talking about their home and lives, watching TV, or Gerald's favourite, going early to his bed for a long night's sleep. This suited Mary. Knowing her teenage charge was safely in his bed left her free to be courted by John Doherty, a handsome young man with a good job.

Gerald was a very caring person. When Mary was sick, he would stay with her, and care for her, just as she would for him. For a time there was no one else. Even though extended family lived nearby, poverty touched every life in the Bogside and relatives had little to give. Mary and Gerald depended on each other, and built a new life together. Visiting Patrick in Portrush (taking time off from seminary to help the family finances) buoyed them and fostered their feeling of family unity.

In 1969, the houses on Wellington Street were slated for demolition. Assisted by an uncle, Mary searched for a new home and chose one at Meehan Square, Maisonette 27-A. Mary and Gerald mourned the loss of their family home, but looked forward to a new beginning, a new chapter in their lives. Six flights up, a trash chute, large living-room with floor-to-ceiling windows, heat on the first floor, two bedrooms and a bathroom up, Mary covered the walls in blue paper with a white frieze. She adored her lovely maisonette. Her first home of her own. Just the right size for Mary and Gerald, with enough space if she and John Doherty decided to marry.

Mary worked for Birmingham Sound Reproducers, a company that produced record changers and employed upwards of 5,000 workers in Derry. However, at the stroke of a pen, the company's owner, Dr MacDonald, closed the doors and moved the operation to Scotland.

Without severance pay and with a teenage boy to feed, Mary promptly went to work in the shirt factories. Gerald started college at Strand Tech but soon decided that working would be better for him and Mary who had struggled to keep food on the table and him in school. He went to work for Carlin's Brewery loading the delivery lorry.

Life was hard. For the first four years after their parents' death, enough money for potatoes and bread was all it took to keep Mary and Gerald happy enough. In 1970, John Doherty joined the household. His presence relieved the loneliness Mary felt. She now had someone to rely on, to help her make decisions. She'd spent four years often not knowing where to turn. Jackie joined Gerald in filling the void in Mary's heart left by her parents' deaths and contributed another income to the household.

As Mary's life grew and changed, Gerald was beginning to gain independence. His job at Carlin's supplied him with an income, confidence, and a growing social life. Just as his father had done with Rebecca, Gerald faithfully turned over his wages to Mary who managed the family finances. She let him keep whatever he wanted or needed and put the rest away for his future.

A stroll into town one spring afternoon changed Gerald's life. Laughing and joking as they walked along, Gerald and his friends looked forward to checking out the girls who would be promenading around the Diamond on the Sunday afternoon. The group of lads ambling into town were crossing the Diamond when two police cars screeched to a halt. The police got out and pointed to Gerald and his friends Gearóid (O'hEara), Eddie, and Charlie. They said, 'You are under arrest for riotous behaviour!' The police claimed the lads had just attacked an RUC car at the bottom of Fahan Street. They had walked up Fahan, but they didn't see or do anything on their journey, including vandalising an RUC vehicle. Only an idiot would vandalise an RUC car so close to the Diamond, which was a haven for the police.

Unbeknownst to them, there had been a bit of a skirmish down Fahan Street, but they were not too worried about the police. They figured it would be resolved. They would have been complete fools to vandalise a police car and then – as a group – continue casually strolling up the street, through the gate, and into the Diamond. They figured the police would realise this and conclude they could not be the culprits.

At Strand Road Barracks, Charlie ended up being thrown out. He was significantly younger than the other boys and his clear distress caused the police to dismiss him. One by one a series of policemen came in to formally identify Gerald, O'hEara, and Eddie, 'Yes, that's definitely the man I saw attacking the car.' O'hEara requested a solicitor and for them to ring his parents which they eventually did. Soon enough, family friend and MP, John Hume arrived.

John informed the boys that the RUC was about to charge them with riotous behaviour, which carried a mandatory sentence of six months. Regardless of their true activities, several policemen signed statements saying they could positively identify them as the people who were at the front of the crowd. Two or three policemen against the lads' word meant they had slim chance of reprieve, but John negotiated and postponed their trial for a week.

Their families paid their bail and the lads got out. After a bit of time weighing up their options – go to prison or go on the run – they decided to take off over the border. It seemed a good idea at the time. They fancied the idea of being desperados on the lam.

They gathered a few contacts – names and addresses of Derry folk – and headed south. Gerald, O'hEara, and Eddie showed up on door-steps and were taken in as family. They earned a few pounds washing windows, doing bar work, day labour, and plaster. The three slept in the same bed, wore the same clothes, earned their few pounds, and missed their families, but mostly it was like a holiday – not like being on the run from the law. After all, nobody was scouring the countryside for them.

They bummed about from town to town seeing the sites, meet-ing girls, and leaving broken hearts, not crime, in their wake. The boy's southern adventure took them through Ennistymon, Shannon, Limerick City, Tipperary, Clonmel, Cashel, Kerry, Killorglin, Clinnon, Cork, and Dublin. Living, working, and playing, they saw more of the south in those six months than most Derry people saw in a lifetime. They frequented pubs like Dirty Nellie's, and Gerald entertained the others with his silly off-key homemade songs but it was really no life for a youngster. The boys eventually tired of it and started thinking of returning home.

Taken to court and sentenced in their absence, O'hEara's solicitor got his charge reduced from riotous behaviour to disorderly behaviour and his result was a three-month suspended sentence and a fine. Gerry and Eddie got six months. This news kept them in the South until they heard that internment had been reintroduced. While in Dublin, which they didn't care for anyway, the lads heard the no-go areas had been re-established and again considered returning home. They thought they could go home and live safely within the no-go area.

The lads returned to Limerick and while staying with a woman named Bridgett, a Derryman, Paddy Brown turned up for a visit and the three desperados asked him for a lift back to Derry. He told them to meet him at Joe Quinn's pub – he was going to have a pint and then they'd be off. He sat and drank until half eleven and then they all got in the car and drove six hours back to Derry.

They arrived to find a dramatically different Derry. Cars were smouldering; CS gas hung in the air; barricades cordoned off the neighbourhood; stones and broken bottles littered the streets. Armed soldiers and civilians patrolled their respective sides of the conflict. Arriving home, their families were more worried than when they were gone. The lads thought their families would be really pleased to see them as they'd left without so much as a nod but they weren't. Derry was on fire.

Gerald, O'hEara, and Eddie got back into the swing of life and started sneaking out. Technically they shouldn't have left the no-go area, but they started sneaking out on a Friday or Saturday night to a pub on Foyle Street. Not that the RUC was out combing the streets for them. The arrival of the British Army, internment, and the no-go area kept the RUC busy enough. The three lads enjoyed their outlaw status nonetheless. There was notoriety in being home from a run from the law in the Free State.

The Metropolitan Bar hung between the Unionist and Nationalist communities and was home to all of Derry – Protestant and Catholic. It was here that Gerald met Hester, a Protestant girl from the Waterside. Hester lived in a very strong Loyalist area and the two Gerrys would walk over to her house together because her neighbourhood was a dangerous place for Catholics. But they were quite daring, being desperados and all.

Gerald got really serious about Hester, decided he was in love with her, and that they were going to get married. But Gerald was on the run and that didn't square with Hester's Protestant background. Her pro-establishment view of the world was that you served your time and then got on with your life. So he did. He decided that he would hand himself in and he got his brother Paddy to walk down with him. His friends and family said their farewells, he walked down to the barricade, and off he went to serve his prison term. It was October 1971.

Gerald arrived in prison and immediately settled in. Having already experienced trauma in his life, he took this temporary change in lifestyle in his stride. A teen with a preference for blue jeans and long hair, Mary didn't recognise him on her first visit. 'Here I am

Mary!' The familiar voice came from a man sporting a dirty pink waistcoat, a wide-collared blue- and white-striped shirt, and short-cropped hair.

Mary received three letters from Gerald during his imprisonment. His words, through his letters, reveal his personality and his plans:

Dear Mary,

I am doing great. I have got my hair cut as you might have guessed. The food is very good and the prisoners are mostly from Belfast. The prison officers treat us very well. I was wondering if you could send someone up to meet me when I get released. Could you send me up a pen, some soap, toothbrush and toothpaste, that is all.

Dear Hester,

Well, I arrived on Wednesday night at about nine o'clock and the time has flown by very quickly. It is Saturday night already. I miss you very much Hester love and the first month I get back we will get engaged. I will have my hair cropped when I am released. Please write as soon as you can but only one letter a month. This is all for now Hester love so goodbye till next time. All my love goes with this letter, Gerry.

Dear Mary,

Just a few lines to let you know that I am keeping well. Thank you very much for the visit. Aunt Annie was up to visit me on the first of this month and left me some cigarette papers and books. I wonder could you send me up a lighter and petrol, also some flints. Also could you send me up a few magazines like *Weekend* or *Reville* and only send up journals not daily papers.

Well this is all for now. P.S. Don't forget the lighter and tell everybody I was asking for them. Love, Gerry.

Dear Mary,

Just a few lines in reply to your letter. I'm sorry I didn't write sooner but you know how it is you kind of forget things. I'll bet you think that I've forgotten about something but I haven't. I wish you a happy anniversary, it's only the first but it won't be the last. No news yet of a bundle of joy some company for Denis or are you thinking about it.

Well how's young Denis keeping does he still keep you awake at night or is he quieter now. I'm sorry I can't be there for the anniversary but I should be there for Christmas. I was wondering could you get me a pair of Wranglers and a Wrangler jacket which is a jean coat with the money in the credit union and get yourself a present and a few drinks on me. What's this about Hester saying I wasn't writing, she mustn't be receiving them. I'll write my last letter to Hester and address it to the factory so that she will get it.

P.S. Don't forget about the jeans coat size 34, trousers 29 make sure that you get the Wranglers. All for now. Best of Luck, Gerry Donaghey.

Gerald was to be in Crumlin Road Prison for six months. If he served his time he'd have been far from harm's way on 30 January 1972. As luck would have it, Ian Paisley was arrested and jailed at Crumlin Road. Paisley's supporters caused such a ruckus outside the prison that the powers that be decided to grant amnesty to everyone serving less than three years thus unburdening themselves and the neighbouring public of the riotous beast and giving a whole host of minor offenders, just-plain-innocents, and their families a happy Christmas gift.

Just before his release date, Mary wrote to Carlin's asking if Gerald could return to work when he got home. The letter she received from the Brewery was not as cheerful as Gerald's correspondence from prison. She was curtly told there was no longer a place for Gerald.

Gerald's letters reveal he was still very much a boy at heart. They certainly don't sound like the letters of a dangerous felon. His big concern is new jeans, 'coat size 34, trousers 29'. But he was finding his way. He had struggled a bit in the previous few years – struggled to find himself, figure out who he was and what he wanted. He'd started college and dropped out to get a job. He worked diligently for Carlin's brewery and attended the training centre. At some point, unbeknownst to Mary, he joined Fianna Eireann but never got the chance to meaningfully participate. His arrest for riotous behaviour was just unlucky and the decision to run off to the South a typical teenager's rash decision.

Even so, Gerald was coming around. His experiences in the south helped him realise that a world existed beyond the Derry walls. His time in Crumlin Road gave him the opportunity to think and evaluate his future. His love for Hester made him want to settle down. Gerald was growing up and becoming a man. When he was released from prison he was ready to step into adulthood and start a new life for himself.

On 29 January 1972, four weeks after Gerald returned home from Crumlin Road, a bullet came through a window and lodged in the wall by the upstairs landing. The occasion was blamed on sporadic violence related to the barracks at Bligh's Lane. Nobody thought it was a sign of something more ominous.

The next day Mary and Gerald would attend a peace march against internment. It was Mary's first march. The people of Derry had made great strides in their quest for civil rights – marching for equal access to housing, jobs, and voting. Marches were designed to be peaceful demonstrations, and although several incidents of violence were perpetrated upon march participants, over the years they typically went off as intended.

Mary put her new boy Denis in his pram and went out to the march on the Sunday 30 January. Halfway through the march Mary decided to take Denis home, get him out of the cold, and prepare tea and sandwiches. Gerald said he would be home for his tea at seven o'clock as he was going to meet his girlfriend at six. It was now just half three, but Mary had some tidying up to do to prepare for the coming week.

At home, Mary cared for her Denis, straightened up around the house, and waited. A wee while passed and then a friend, Kathleen Flood, called at the door. She asked was there anyone home with Mary? She then told Mary that she heard Gerald had been shot in the leg. To her relief, Mary soon learned that it wasn't Gerald that had been shot.

Unfortunately, Mary's cousin Damian was the victim. Seven o'clock came and went and Mary began to worry. She felt guilty about feeling relief it was Damien shot and not her Gerald. But where was Gerald?

More rumours of Gerald being shot prompted Mary's husband to go over to Altnagelvin Hospital to find Gerald. Jackie made several trips between home and hospital that night only to be told Gerald was not there. The waiting was terrible. Mary hoped there was a mistake, that he was with his girl and had simply lost track of time. She prayed. It just wasn't possible that another member of her family would be so tragically taken away. He must be alive. Her emotions changed from hope to despair. She tried to remain positive, but the hours ticked by and fear of the worst crept in. Gerald's friends came to the house and reported that Gerald had been shot. But it wasn't until Father Rooney arrived that Mary knew with certainty that Gerald was dead.

Gerald's body was not delivered to hospital until ten o'clock that evening. John's final journey to hospital that day was to identify Gerald. He returned home heavy-hearted, charged with a terrible task – telling Mary that another member of her close-knit family was dead. Together Gerald and Mary had grown stronger after the sudden and tragic loss of their parents. They had survived and built a lovely life together. It was good. And then, it was over. A quiet pall came over the house. For the third time in her twenty-four years, Mary contacted Patrick to report a death in their family.

Gerald's body came home Monday night. In the twenty-four hours he was home, the house never emptied. It seemed as if all of Derry stepped out to wake its dead. Thousands of people moved from house to house offering solace to as many families as they could reach. On Tuesday, caskets containing the bodies of the men and boys murdered by the British Paratroopers were delivered to St Mary's chapel streaming down from Creggan and up from the Bogside all through the evening. Gerald's body, tucked quietly in to the shining wooden casket, was carried to the chapel by his closest friends and family. And then, Mary was alone.

It was months before Mary learned the whole story of her brother's death: Gerald had been shot running for home. He was cut down while seeking safety from the reckless firing of soldiers who had been ordered to cease fire. Gerald was wounded, but the injury was not imminently fatal. He was alive and likely to survive with prompt and proper medical attention. Two men, Leo Young and Raymond Rogan, lifted Gerald into a car and raced toward Altnagelvin Hospital, determined to save his life. Despite his desperation in not being able to find his own brother, Leo held Gerald in the back seat, talking to him, comforting him, urging him to hold on.

British soldiers stopped the car and Leo and Mr Rogan were dragged out, their lives threatened. The car with Gerald in the back seat was driven away and the men were arrested. Gerald lay alone in the back seat of the Cortina, his life slowly ebbing away. When Leo Young was released two days later, he would learn his brother John was also murdered.

Mary left the maisonette at Meehan Square in Easter of 1972. Unable to continue living in the house so close to where Gerald was shot, she took a house in Carnhill. One night shortly after moving, Mary saw Gerald. Sleeping in the front room she woke up with the feeling someone was there. Gerald stood dressed in his Wranglers and shirt with the orange and fine green stripe going down it. He stood there, just as he always had, hands shoved in his pockets, relaxed, smiling. He looked at Mary for a moment and then, he was gone.

Patrick is now a priest in America and Mary lives in her home in Carnhill. She and Jackie have lovely children who would have adored their Uncle Gerald, just as he adored his first nephew, Denis. Mary survives her father Charles, her mother Rebecca, and her dear brother Gerald.

Each died too young, lost to tragic circumstance. But it is Gerald's death that tears at her soul. Shot and left to die alone in the back seat of a car hijacked by British soldiers, what was Gerald thinking in his last hours of life? How long did he lie in that car before he took his last breath? Did he wonder why his sister didn't come to him? Why his family wasn't there to help him? Why he'd been left alone? Mary prays he was granted peace at his death; that the pain from his wounds was masked; that he was gone when they handled his body and planted the nail-bombs so he didn't suffer that further violation and pain. Gerald's visit to Mary's room offered her comfort in the knowledge that Gerald has been granted peace in the arms of his creator. Mary's peace will come when her brother's name is cleared.

Michael Kelly

Saw poor Mrs Kelly down the town today,
she's suffering so, yer heart just breaks for her.[27]

The seventh child of thirteen,[28] Michael Kelly was seventeen when he was shot and killed while standing near the Rossville Street barricade. William Nash, John Young, and Michael McDaid fell moments after Michael went down. All well-dressed young men, headed for the safety of the barricade. That was their refuge. The army never went past the barricade. Michael was wearing a blue suit and yellow jumper. He had a half-eaten chocolate bar in his pocket. Sunday wasn't the day for rioting. The boys were out for the craic.

Mrs Kelly knew Michael better than anyone else. I would have loved to listen to her tell her son's story but she had a stroke in 2004. As her family gathered around her with love and support, her son John took the time to share her story.

We were just like everyone else. We had very little. My father was unemployed. There were twelve children around the house, so there was a lot of to-ing and fro-ing.

My mother was the mainstay. She reared the children. She didn't drink. She didn't smoke. She was very religious. My father was the opposite. Like every Derry man he had his pint and did his wee bit of smoking. So it was down to my mother to ensure that the wains were looked after and brought up right.

What my mother did was a miracle. Bringing up that many children was a lot of heavy work. She was a normal Derry woman. She looked after her children, brought us up correctly, taught us to respect our elders, and to do what we were told. As a result, there were very few occasions that we had to be chastised because we showed respect to everyone.

It was a struggle on a daily basis to feed all of us. For example, today people take chicken for granted. In those days we had chicken only at Christmas. I remember going to school and travelling home at lunchtime. It was a two-mile round trip for just a slice of bread, but it was adequate, because we knew we'd be getting dinner when we got home. And my mother always had the dinner on the table.

In those days, you knew what kind of dinner you were going to get. It never changed. You got your soup and spuds on the Sunday. Reheated soup, which I hated, with spuds on the Monday. Stew on Tuesday. I hate stews now. She always put turnips into it and I hate turnips. Wednesday and Thursday were typically centred on spuds and Friday we had fish. In the morning it was porridge. There was no such thing as cornflakes, cornflakes didn't exist in those days, or maybe they were too expensive, I don't know, but they never came into our house. That was more or less how we lived at the time. My mother ran clubs to earn money. This meant she collected payment from people who bought things on tick from the shops. She earned a small commission and that was what she had to feed and clothe twelve children as well as keep up the house.

My father was one of these guys who didn't have steady work. Then at one time he did get a steady job and things were grand! He cycled from Creggan to the Waterside, but he worked at night so he had time for a few pints during the day. So, when I say cycle, it's a relative term. He leaned on the bike to get into work and back again – like Lee Marvin and his white horse. He was a man, a typical Derry man with the drink, that's all I'm saying.

For my mother it was all about her wains, all about the house, all about rearing them and bringing them up right, and that's exactly what she achieved. No matter what the problems were or what was thrown in front of her, she'd look after her children first. It was always a massive undertaking for her and she achieved it. She created a good family.

At that time we all left school at fifteen and went to work. Every Friday we handed our unopened wage packets to our mother. But we only worked for four or five years and then got married, so my mother had only four or five years of each of us handing in a wage packet. The boys worked at what ever we could find and the girls, every one of them, worked in a shirt factory, which was the only

work for the majority of the people in the city at the time.

It was important that you went straight home on the Friday and handed in your wage packet. You didn't give it to your da. You gave it to your mother. She looked after the money. She looked after the main running of the house. Everyone was the same. Every child was expected to turn over their pay.

It certainly was a struggle in those days. We had nothing. It was a massive undertaking for my mother to buy a TV but she saved and she did it. In fact, we were the first on our street to get a TV and all the wains came up to the window to see it. The sum of our amenities was a TV, a record player, and a radio. But we were happy. Maybe even happier in those days than people are today because we were such a close family.

My mother worried about her boys. Work was hard to come by in Derry and as we reached our teenage years, the Troubles were starting. She didn't want us involved in anything. She wanted us to learn a trade and get jobs. She knew her boys would have to be responsible for a family and she wanted her boys to be good providers.

At the time girls got married, had children, and depended on their husbands to be the breadwinners. Our mother was happy with that as long as the girls got jobs to help cover their expenses until they were married and out of the house. In fact, my mother would have worried more about her boys than the girls because at the end of the day she knew where her girls were and what they were doing. She knew the girls would get married and start a family. But the boys had a multitude of distractions, and she worried, 'Would they end up on the dole? Get mixed up in the Troubles? Become drinkers? Struggle all through their lives?'

That was the way she was, but in saying that everyone in our house was treated completely and utterly fairly. If she came into the house with a packet of sweets, everybody got one. If you got two, I got two. Everything was shared equally. She never singled anyone out at all. If she spent money on a pair of shoes, the next person coming along would have the same amount of money spent on them. If a dress was bought, the same amount of money was spent on the next dress, and so on.

My mother always put her family first. She protected her family. She looked after the family very, very well. I look upon my mother as a Derry woman, which to me is a woman who takes joy in bringing up a family. My mother took joy in bringing up our family, and I think she took even more joy at the fact that we all turned out well.

Derry mothers in relation to their sons: I think I can say Derry mothers think the sun shines out of everyone of their arses, to put it crudely! I think they see their sons as doing no wrong at all, unless, of course it is something extreme. That's the way my mother was. As far as she was concerned she brought us up right. She expected us to behave ourselves and to give respect to everyone.

She was my hero, if you want to call it that. She was a wee woman who took it upon her shoulders to rear a family and she achieved a good family. Just look at her now, she's still there and still fighting even after a major stroke, she is still with us – her family. As far as I'm concerned, that's a Derry woman, and a good woman. Your family comes first.

Michael was a quiet soul. When he was three years of age he fell into a coma. The morning he became ill my mother came in and had us all kneel round his bed and say the Rosary before he was taken away in the ambulance.

My mother was a very religious person. She went to Mass every morning until she lost the use of her legs. But I remember that

morning. We were told to pray for him, that he'd come round. I think he was in the hospital for about three weeks, and we weren't even allowed to go in and see him. He was in a ward of his own, and he went into a deep sleep. I think it was a virus of some sort he'd picked up that affected the brain. My mother was told to offer him up to God, but she refused to do it. She said, 'No! I'm going to pray for him.' She prayed steadfastly until he was well. My mother has a great belief in the power of prayer. She prayed and Michael came back to us.

My memories of Michael are few between that time and when he went to work. I was seven years older than he and so to me he was just a brother. I know my mother helped him build a large pigeon loft out in the backyard. She helped to get him the wood and all the pigeons, too.

When he was working in Derry, he would take a couple of pigeons down to his work and release them, and she would wait for them to fly back. Then, when he was in Belfast my ma cared for the pigeons while he was away during the week, feeding them, exercising them, and making sure they stayed well. It was almost as if by looking after those pigeons she was watching after Michael.

My mother looked after Michael so closely she actually followed him on the march. She saw him a few times and was more or less trying to keep an eye on him. I think when the march got to William

Street, she lost track of him so she went to her sisters flat in Kells Walk. She maintains that she looked out the door into Colmcille Court, and saw Michael running along as the Paras moved in. She called to him but he didn't hear her, and that was the last time she saw him alive.

Much later she learned that she was directly above the wall where Soldier F fired, so Michael's murderer was directly below her and that fact was devastating to her. Here she was taking shelter oblivious to what was happening to her son just below.

We held a wake in the house. Thousands of people came to give condolences. Even an ex-RUC man came in, devastated, and admitted that the men and boys were murdered.

My mother was heavily sedated but on the Tuesday in the early

hours of the morning she lifted Michael from his coffin and hugged him. She was crying and saying, 'Michael son, Michael son'. We had to restrain her and put Michael back into the coffin.

Michael's death affected my mother very badly. We were a very close family. My mother could not find a way of coping with his death and we were very worried about her for many years. She regularly went to the RUC Station on the Strand Road to remonstrate and had to be calmed down by Superintendent Lagan.

One winter we found my mother in the cemetery with a blanket trying to keep Michael warm at his grave. My mother had a nervous breakdown after Michael's death. She has no memory of the five years after Michael's death. She just existed.

We all saw our mother suffering, but we never knew the pain our da felt until he died, when we found a wallpaper sample book filled with twenty-one years of Bloody Sunday newspaper clippings and photos of Michael. He was a typical Derry man to the end – he suffered in silence.

Our ma kept Michael's clothes, the Mars bar she gave him every week before he returned to Belfast, and a half-eaten Whole Nut chocolate bar he had in his pocket the day of the march. She's up the stairs now, a year after her stroke, having good days and bad. When she goes, she'll take the last of Michael's physical remains with her. She will be buried with his clothes. She would have done it if it was anyone of us killed. In our house everything is shared equally, especially the love.[29]

Barney McGuigan

Fifty-four people witnessed Barney McGuigan's murder.
All fifty-four people saw the same thing:
Barney McGuigan stepped out with his hands raised over his head,
waving a white handkerchief.

Barney McGuigan was a husband. Barney and his wife had six children and were very happy together. They were an extremely good team, dividing the running of the household between them. Bernie took care of the day-to-day running of the household cooking, cleaning, baking, knitting, and making dresses for their daughters. Barney earned a living at the Ben Sherman shirt factory and Birmingham Sound Reproducers. They were a couple totally in love, whose children never witnessed an argument between them. Over thirty years after Barney's death, his wife is still in his corner. She kept their family together after his death and remembers him fondly to their children.

Barney McGuigan was a family man. He placed a lot of importance on family and family relationships. Family was something he valued tremendously. He was home in the evenings and regularly took his eldest son to Derry City football matches. He planned for his children to be well-educated and attend university. The McGuigan home always had an open door. Barney and Bernie encouraged their children to bring their friends home. Barney had an exceptional singing voice. His children heard him singing in the house regularly. The McGuigan children lived in a happy house with happy parents who made them feel very safe and secure.

Barney McGuigan was a dedicated employee. During his tenure at BSR, he was promoted to charge-hand. As charge-hand Barney

was responsible for twelve men. A dedicated worker, his section was very efficient and required little oversight. There were never any complaints from Barney's section nor word of any problems. Barney was a very quiet and soft-spoken man. Because of this he was well-liked and respected by the men who worked for him. When Ben Sherman's shirts revolutionised the shirt-making industry in Derry, Barney was involved in constructing the expansion of their Abercorn Road factory. He was very affable and got along well with the other employees, most of whom were women.

Barney McGuigan was an important member of the community. He represented young people in housing. He was involved in the Tenants' Association. He interacted with the housing executive to ensure the neighbourhood was maintained and there were lights on in the area. Barney called on the fathers in the district to stop stone-throwing near the primary school and to try to restore some semblance of discipline to the local teenagers and to improve their behaviour. Forty fathers attended a meeting set up by Barney and organised themselves to take care of the school to prevent any further damage to it. They did their very best to bring the stone-throwing to an end and eventually did so.

Barney McGuigan didn't look for glory or recognition. All the things he did to help people he did very quietly. Only a week or two before he was killed he went out to take up a collection for a family who were getting their electricity cut off. He found shoes for shoeless children, took collections for families in need, worked as a community liaison between families and the government housing association, and advocated for children to have safe passage to and from school. Barney told his children, 'If you do something to help someone you don't need to publicise it and you don't need a pat on the back for doing it.'

Barney McGuigan was held in high regard. He could tell a joke and enjoyed the craic with his friends. If someone confided in Barney, they knew it would remain confidential. People who were having a problem, such as their electricity getting turned off, were quite happy to talk to him about it knowing that was as far as it went. Barney was outgoing and had a good personality and enjoyed a bit of fun. He was always concerned for people experiencing difficulties and if he was in a position to help them he did. Barney's friends, both

Protestant and Catholic, visited the house where they enjoyed time together. They speak of Barney fondly to this day.

Barney McGuigan was a good neighbour. The summer before he died a friend of his asked him could he make a headstone for this fella's mother who had died? This particular family couldn't afford a headstone at the time and so Barney made the headstone in his back yard. As the McGuigan's lived overlooking the cemetery, Barney and his sons took it down and placed it at the woman's grave. As a result, Barney was inundated with people who wanted a stone. Before he died, Barney made nine in all. The nine headstones stand in the City Cemetery today. Made in the McGuigan backyard – free of charge.

Barney McGuigan was compassionate. If Barney had stayed by the phone box he would probably have survived Bloody Sunday. But he heard Paddy Doherty crying for help so he took a hanky, waved it and said, 'They won't shoot me. I've got to go help this man,' as he stepped out to go to Paddy's side. Barney didn't believe he was going to be shot. He had six children and at forty-one years of age had his whole life before him. On Bloody Sunday Barney's compassion led him to go to the aid of a dying man. For his compassion he was shot through the head. With his compassion he laid down his life for another.

Kevin McElhinney

Kevin McElhinney was a responsible young man. He worked for Lipton's
supermarket from the time he finished school and never missed a day.
He had a keen interest in soccer and athletics but his real passion was
music. At the time of his death he was learning to drive and was saving
for a car of his own.

Kevin McElhinney's family was unable to participate in the development of this book.

William McKinney

He seems to have been roughly the most boring man on the march. His temperament was mild in the extreme. He didn't go drinking or stoning the army, didn't even do any dancing.[30]

The kitchen is where many of us find our fondest childhood memories. It was the place we rushed through and slammed the back door a hundred times a day. Where warm biscuits were produced and love was doled out. In the McKinney house, like many others in Derry, it was the centre of life, where the meals were prepared, the washing done, the shirts ironed, and for the better part of her life, the kitchen was the only place you would find Mrs McKinney.

Ten children, a husband, the granda, sisters, and assorted friends and neighbours dropping by kept her kitchen open from sunrise to sunset. The McKinney kitchen opened on to the alley, where Granda got hit by the car and Willie locked Peter in the shed.

Mrs McKinney's sharp mind and activity belie her eighty-four years.[31] She's always out and about, 'George comes on a Wednesday night and he comes on a Sunday night; Ann comes on a Wednesday night; Patrick comes on a Friday night; and Peter comes on a Thursday night. They all run me to bingo, and they all come back for me, I take another woman that lives up the street, and we go to bingo. Peter runs me down to the Marian Hall and George collects me. Patrick runs me to the Stardust on a Tuesday night, Peter runs me on a Thursday night, and Kathleen runs me on a Monday night and Joe collects me. They all take turn about. Oh they're wile good'. Kathleen says, 'She's a better life than I have at night! We have to book now when we're coming in. She's always out at bingo!'

Daily Mrs McKinney sits in her chair by the front window of 62 Westway where she has lived for forty-six years. The window overlooks the green where her children played. It overlooks the footpath to the front door where hundreds of mourners queued to pay their respects when Willie was murdered. Mrs McKinney's chair faces the fireplace – the same wall where Willie hung a sheet and entertained the family with Mickey Mouse cartoons on his first film projector – and, of course, there's a view of the kitchen.

From her chair she tells stories of her children. Stories of Willie and George: brothers, eleven months apart but different as night and day; Granda, whose antics cause Mrs McKinney to roll her eyes and chuckle; Willie's loves: his first teacher, his work, his fiancée, music, and photography. She told me about those who loved Willie most: Joanna who fell for the first-born baby as she walked the floors, cradling him in her arms; Elizabeth, who loved Willie for six years, patiently waiting for the day they would be married; the grandchildren who never got to meet their uncle, but who no doubt would have loved him just as he adored his first darling niece.

A patient, kind, and generous family, they shared Willie's life. A life filled with passion and dedication. At twenty-seven, his was a life just beginning to blossom: a good job, lovely wife-to-be, search for his first house underway, and growing talent in photography. Come into the house. Sit. Have a cup of tea and listen. Mrs McKinney will tell you about her son:

Willie was born on 27 February 1944. Each and every one of them was born at home. But Willie, George, and Kathleen were born in my sister's house at 36 Saint Columb's Wells. Willie, George, and Kathleen used to say, 'I was born in the Wells you know.' St Columb is the patron saint of Derry and the Wells were the heart of the Bogside (even before it was the Bogside) so being born there is an honour.

As a baby, Willie never slept. We walked the floor with him at night. During the day Joanna wrapped him in her shawl and walked him around town. At the weekend, Granda tucked him in his pram and walked him down the quay. He wasn't fussy. He just always wanted up out of the cot. When George was born, their father was raging, he thought we had Willie spoiled, because George slept away.

But Willie never slept his whole life. If he wasn't up late work-ing at the *Journal* office he was developing pictures or lying awake listening to his wireless. Many a night I went into his room and he'd have it to his ear listening to everything that was going on down the town. Thinking he was sleeping, I would go to pull it out, and he'd say, 'Let that alone.'

After Kathleen was born we moved to 6 Orchard Lane. Orchard Lane was where Willie started school. Miss Johnston was Willie's first teacher. Willie's primary school was one street over from our house on Orchard Lane and Willie would come home and say things like, 'Miss Johnston sent me, could you lend her an egg?' No matter what Miss Johnston wanted, she sent Willie round for it. And I would say, 'Have they nothing in that school at all?'

There was a place at the bottom of the street where the rough crowd ran about and a place at the top of the street where the reserved crowd hung out. George's pals came from the bottom of the street and Willie's from the top. This woman, they called her Mrs Rabbit, used to come into the lane and shout, 'Mrs McKinney take this George! He's keeping all these ones going down here!'

One day George went with Willie's friends over to a carpark to learn how to ride a bike. There was a crowd that came from the far end of town to pick fights with Willie's choir crowd. So they asked George, would he come learn to ride the bike with them? He didn't

know he was being set up. They invited him along knowing the crowd was going to come and fight with them and that George would take care of them. The crowd turned up, George turned on the crowd, and Willie and his friends had no bother after. So even if they didn't run around together, Willie and George's relationship had utility.

Willie and George took turns working in a fish shop. The proprietors couldn't wait for George to finish school and find another job, but they loved Willie. They near enough wanted to adopt him. They had a room ready and all. When we moved from town up to Creggan, the wife sent up word to see would we let Willie stay the weekend? She said it was very late for him to go home, and they had a spare room. So I said to him, 'Are you going to stay?' He says, 'I don't want to stay, I want to come home at night.' So he came up at night.

At the bottom of the street where all the roughs were, there woulda been footballin' or stealin' or down the quay makin trouble. Four priests come out of the top of the street crowd. When we left Orchard Lane the lads that Willie was pals with lit a bonfire 'cause George was leaving. Mrs Rabbit said, 'Oh I am glad to see the back of that young fella. All he did was fight down here. He'da fought with his shadow.' Willie and George only fought once. Caught fighting in the street by their da – it didn't take much for him to convince them that wouldn't be tolerated. So George went on to fight another lad, another day and Willie went back to his small group of quiet friends.

Willie took an early interest in music and took piano accordion lessons. He practiced up the stairs here. You can see from the window here that there are three buildings around the grassy square. Well, in those buildings someone played a trumpet and another played the drums so between Willie and what was going on across the green, all of Westway could hear the music.

Willie used to take his accordion along to play on bus runs – which were outings with the Hibernians or the men from work. One night I saw him coming up the back alley with the accordion. He said to me, 'You think I am coming up here drunk.' And I said no, but of course I did.

But Willie didn't turn out that way. If it was George and somebody said to me, 'Where's George?' It woulda been George is down at the club or George is pegging stones or he's away playing football or table tennis. You'd always known what George was about but Willie was a quiet fella. He minded his own business. He was private about his own life for the most part. Willie would have been interested if something happened or somebody wanted to tell him something. If something went on, he'd enquire about it, but ordinarily he went his own quiet way and bothered about nobody.

Their Granda lived with us on Orchard Lane until he died and he contributed his own brand of chaos to the mix. The wains would go up the stairs to their beds and Granda would call down, 'I can't get to sleeping with all these wains! They're wild!' Well that was some going! Sometimes it was wild, the carry on, it was desperate! Whoever lay on the bottom bunk pulled down the bottom sheet through the spring, and then the pillows were getting flung. The Granda would shout, 'They're going to kill me up here! I can't get sleeping with these ones carrying on!' But it was him winding them up!

Granda was a fowl-plucker. The boys visited him at work and knew about the big fridge that kept the chickens cold. They called the shop owner Wiggy on account of his baldness! The wains would be washing and warming themselves by the oil fire at night and Granda, lying in the back room you see, would shout out again, 'They're going to kill me up here.' And they would say, 'Aye this is like Wiggy's fridge!' Granda would say, 'They're killing me. They brought me out of Wiggy's fridge!

This is like Wiggy's fridge!' And then they all laughed and carried on, and then they all got a hiding, and it was Granda keeping them going! Sometimes it was wild you know – they were all at one another.

There were only two places Granda could work and that was either the shop on Carlisle Road or the one on Ferryquay Street. So if he wasn't in the one he was in the other. George and Willie used to get money off the Granda for the matinee. So they would go to the shop and ask the man who owned the shop, 'Is our Granda in?' and he would say, 'Aye, he's in the back.'

The Granda would be in a little room at the back with one hundred, maybe two hundred chickens. He'd see the lads and say, 'How youse know I was here?' Willie and George said, 'Well, we just knew' and hold their hands out for money. They went to the Rialto and soon enough we would all be looking for them. We were worried sick and they'd be lying sleeping in the Rialto.

Granda loved the wains in his own way. He walked Willie and George in their prams down the quay. He handed out money to the boys. When Kathleen was small he took her shopping down the town. At home he let her powder his face. I would come in from the shopping and she'd have him all made up.

He was a character and we missed him sorely when he died. He was coming home one night and a car knocked him down. Apparently the driver was speeding, and he knocked him some thirty or forty yards when he hit him. The damage was mostly to his legs. One of the feet had to come off, and he would say to Mickey, 'How am I going to walk home from Altnagelvin? How am I going to get home with only one leg?' The nurses were wild about him. They brought him beer and took good care of him. But the day came when they rang and when Mickey went over Granda was dead.

My sister Joanna was wild about Willie, too. She walked him when he was a baby and later took him, George, and Kathleen on a summer holiday. Joanna and her friend Lily took Willie all over the island. George and Kathleen would have gone along at the summer but it was Willie they were attached to and they took him everywhere. Joanna and Lily took the three to Buncrana, Malin Head, and Bundoran from the time they were seven or eight until they left school and went to work. That was a gift to me. With those three gone I only had seven left to deal with and that was a holiday for me too. When they went to the Free

State, they could get things cheaper so when George got homesick they wrapped fabric around him under his clothes, put a label on him, and put him on the bus for home.

We moved to Creggan when Willie was fourteen. At that time he worked at a chemist shop in William Street. He didn't like that job at all. Every time he came into this kitchen after his work he cried about it, and I would ask, 'What's wrong?'

'I don't like it.'

'And why do you not like it?'

'Because it's all women work in it, and I would rather work with men.'

Joanna pleaded his case to his father. She came up on the Sunday night and Willie would be sitting here and Joanna would say, 'How are you getting on in the chemist Willie?'

'I don't like it.'

'You don't like it?'

'No.'

'Why Willie?'

'I don't like working with women.'

'You don't like working with women?'

Joanna would turn to his father, 'See here Mickey. You gonna do something about this young fella? Get him outta that chemist.'

Luckily, a friend of mine met me at Joanna's one Sunday and says, 'How's the family doing?' I says alright, but I got a young fella breaking his heart down at that chemist. So my friend says, 'Wait till I tell you this – I have a grandson leaving the *Derry Journal* office. Tell your son to go down in the morning and see if he can get into it.' So Willie and his father went down in the morning and the *Journal* said the job is only running messages. Willie says, 'I don't care. I'll run the messages as long as I get in with men.'

So he got the job and they liked him and he liked the job and soon he was bringing home a big typewriter to practice as they were training him to become a compositor. He brought a big keyboard home to practice and it wasn't long before he was off the messages and typesetting the paper. He worked steady. Monday and Tuesday nights until four or five in the morning setting the paper for the Tuesday and Friday. When he came in from work on the Monday and Friday he brought five or six *Journals* for relatives, which his brother Mickey delivered: one next door, one to the Wells, one to the fountain, one up the street, one to Joanna, and one to Lily.

One night the father got onto Kathleen about coming in late. The father was very strict about the time, and then he was terrified because Kathleen was going with a Yank. He was afraid the Yank would just take Kathleen away and that's all woulda been about her. So she was late one night and she came in and he checked her about coming in so many minutes late. Willie came in behind her and the father says, 'And that goes for you too.'

Willie said, 'No way. No way am I coming in early. I work at the *Journal* office until two or three in the morning. I go with a girl who lives on the Waterside and I have to leave her off. I don't know what time I'm gonna get in. I'll go and get a flat.' That was awful for me. I said now Willie you don't need to go get a flat. You stay here. And that was that. It got Kathleen off the hook too. The father had plenty to be worried about with the Troubles and all, but these wains were twenty-three and twenty-five then. But their father was right about one thing, Kathleen married the Yank. When they left Derry, Willie posted the *Journal* to her every few weeks.

Willie's late-night walk home from the Waterside meant he saw all that was going on down the town. He would have walked up Great James Street and cut through the park to come home. One night as he crossed Waterloo Street, he found himself between a group of kids running up and the army coming down the street. He was scooped along with the rest of them but when he and his father went to court, they explained Willie's hands were black from his work as a typesetter at the *Journal* office, not from pegging stones, and they let him go.

My husband was Michael McKinney, but all he got was Mickey. I met him at a dance in 1939. We were married in the Long Tower Chapel in 1943. I was twenty-four and he was twenty-one, and he played on that. He says to Mary one night, 'Mary when your mother dies I'm going to get a big blonde in here, and you call her Mummy!' He went in front of me anyway. He was sixty-three when he died.

Life was hard at first. Mickey worked steady but one income with all these children was hard. We had seven when we moved to Creggan. I thought I was finished – but then there was Patrick and Peter and then John. It was wild at times up here with all the children in the house.

I once went to Lourdes with some friends and they were all sitting waiting on me when I came in. Mickey was left with the wains and when we came back he says, 'I never was as glad to see anybody coming back in my life.' My daughter Ann said 'He came over to me and said, "I wish to God I could see your mother back, my brain's turning with them crowd."' Not only was he glad to see me, the wains were glad to see me. They had eaten all their meals from the chip shop while I was gone. I left the meat and spuds out for him but when I came back it was still sitting. I said, Mickey, you didn't cook for them? He says, 'They didn't want it. They all went out and bought outside.'

I was in this kitchen morning, noon, night. Cooking, feeding, and washing dishes while Peter kept the whole lot going. When the television was on he wouldn't let the rest of them listen to it, all I could hear was, 'Ma come on in to Peter!' It was just wild. I never got out again.

That Peter fella called Willie, 'Specky'. When Willie went out the back door, to leave for work at the *Journal* office, the bike was left out the back you see, Peter would call, 'Bye Specky.' And I would say to Willie, Go on and give him a skite! Don't let him call you that. But sooner than give Peter a skite, he'd lift him and carry him out and put him in the shed. There was a bolt on the door, so he bolted him in and said to me, 'As soon as I'm away, let him out.'

It wasn't long till Peter needed glasses too. One day I was here and the nurse comes up and says, 'Peter just got glasses and he can't see the board.' So I took him to the doctor and the doctor says, 'Let me see your glasses.' He took out a cloth and cleaned them off. Peter had been sticking them in his pocket as soon as he left the house, and they were so dirty he couldn't see the board. But he wasn't the only one to take his glasses off. I once found a photo of Willie at a dance. There he was dancing without his glasses. I don't know how he ever danced without glasses. He couldn't see a thing.

Willie had a country and western record collection, and he bought a big music centre to listen to the records. It had two big speakers and took up the corner of the living room beneath the stairs. One night George broke the centre – we don't know what he did but it wouldn't play and I said, Oh, George, they'll be murder when Willie gets home! Well, we sat up shakin', waiting for him to come home. He came in and said, 'Look at youse. What's wrong? There's something wrong.' I said George broke the record centre. Willie said, 'It'll be alright' and he turned and went up to bed.

Willie was sensitive to other people's feelings. He didn't approve of gossip. If the young-uns were talking about someone, he would say, 'Where did you hear that? You don't know if that's true.' He made sure his younger brothers and sisters finished their homework. He told them to get home if they were out. He was quiet but he was principled, and if you were wrong – he would tell you.

One night when Willie and I were chatting in the kitchen, he told me he remembered how much I baked when we lived down the lane. We had a range there and it was wile handy to bake in. When we moved to Creggan, I didn't bake anymore. With so many wains, I just didn't have time. So one Sunday night he's sitting here talking to me and says, 'Go on try a scone.' I said, Willie, it's that long since I done one, I couldn't. He says, 'Go on try it. I'll watch the timing so it doesn't get too hot.' We tried it. It was like a pancake! We had to throw it out!

Willie talked to me in this kitchen, but he was quiet about his personal life. My sister came into me one Sunday evening and said, 'You'll never believe who I saw today going up Shipquay Street with a girl.'

'Who?'

'Willie.'

'My God, I can't believe that.'

'Aye, I saw him. He even looked over at me.'

That was Elizabeth. She lived on the Waterside. He was wild about that girl. She was all he'd have talked about then. One morning I came down the stairs, as usual I was up early, and when I came into the house, what was going round the house but a rabbit! Oh my God! And I went up the stairs and said Willie, you were the last in, did you let in a rabbit? And the mess with it! He says 'No. I bought that for

Elizabeth.' Well, I said, get on now and go take it to Elizabeth! He bought her a rabbit! She loved rabbits and he bought her one.

Elizabeth was the last girl Willie went with. They were together for six years. They were supposed to get married but they never did. George even put off his wedding waiting for them to get married. But then George got tired of waiting so he went ahead.

Willie was camera-mad. His first camera was a small projector. He hung a sheet in the living-room and we all sat on the floor watching black and white Mickey Mouse cartoons. His next camera was a small Pentax 35mm. He was always after me with that camera. He took pictures of me washing socks, cooking dinner, watching television, and many with my hand covering my face. Everywhere I went there was Willie with that camera. I used to try to chase him away. After the camera, seems like all he done was take my photo. He developed his film here at night. When we were all in bed and the house was dark, he stayed up developing all those photos.

He also loved taking pictures of Kathleen's daughter, Elaine. He snapped her photo when she was a baby bouncing in her chair and as she toddled up the footpath and through the gate. Every time he took her picture, he said 'She's powerful!'

His first film was of Elaine. We were all sitting here on a Sunday night and here comes Willie with a light and his movie camera. We were all sitting around Elaine as she played in her wee bouncer and he filmed us playing with her. While the rest of the family sometimes grew weary of his cameras, the wee-one never tired of her uncle Willie taking pictures.

When he got his first movie camera, he began filming all the civil-rights marches. He would get in as close as he could to take in whatever was going on. He filmed the funerals, including the funeral of Sammy Devenney who was beaten to death by the RUC. He filmed the baton charges of the RUC. When they came at him, he didn't move. He stayed on filming. His brothers had to pull him out of the way. He wanted to stay to the last second. He'd be getting a battering to get all the action.

When Willie left for the march, he had his movie camera over his shoulder. I said to Mary, they'll think our Willie's a reporter today, nothing will happen to him. It was only a march, you know, for civil rights. But that was the next of it then, you know.

Willie saw two of his sisters on the way to the march. He pretended to film them as they mugged for the camera and then he sent them home. He tucked his camera under his coat to protect it when the army opened fire. But it was him who needed protecting. The army murdered him as he took cover, crawling by a low wall, crouching in the grass. A woman who saw him just before he was shot said he looked absolutely terrified.

There was a Dr McClean that was with Willie for the last. He went over to him and Willie said, 'Doctor am I going to get better?' Dr McClean says, 'I told that fella a wee white lie, I said, "The ambulance is coming now and they'll take you to Altnagelvin and you'll be all right." It's wile lonely when you're dying, so I held his hand until he died.'

Willie suffered two gunshot wounds. One bullet entered the right side of his back and ripped through his tenth right rib, the lower lobe of his right lung, severed his liver, stomach, colon, and spleen, and broke his left sixth and seventh ribs before exiting his lower left chest. The bullet that hit his left arm left a gaping wound, 8cm x 3cm, on the back of his forearm. The pathology experts say it is unknown whether the wounds came from one bullet or two, but it doesn't really matter, the army shot him in the back and killed him. He was just there to film the march and they shot him.

Willie used to meet Elizabeth at the Guildhall, and the day that it happened she was standing waiting on him. We had to go down and tell her. She waited six years for him to be ready to marry. But they didn't get there. There's honour in being a widow. It must be hard to be the girlfriend of a murder victim. It's easy for people to disregard the depth of the relationship when you are just 'the girlfriend'. But to us she was his fiancée and so, part of our family. He loved her so much. We were so happy for her when she found love again, married, and had a family.

Miss Johnston came to the house for the wake. She was so sad. She must be nearly ninety now, but she still waves over to me at the Long Tower Chapel every Sunday at eleven o'clock Mass.

Kathleen was in Puerto Rico when Willie died. She arrived in Derry the day after the funeral. They held Willie's body back at the chapel and buried him the next day. I thought I was going to the cemetery the day Willie was buried. But that big car pulled up out there for me and I said, I think I am going to his wedding with the like of this car. I couldn't go. I used to go up on cemetery Sunday, but it's a long time since I've been up there. I won't go near it.

We never talked about Willie after he was shot. There were six sons left, and we were afraid they would have got into bother with a soldier or something you know, so we never talked about Willie. But one night they were all sitting, you see, after Willie died, and the father says to them, 'Are any of you in anything?' He meant the IRA. And they said no. He said, 'Well keep it like that, for one sore heart's enough, we don't want any more.'

The story ends. Mrs McKinney sobs. The shrieking, piercing, wounded cry of a mother grieving for her son. It makes your blood run cold and your heart ache. What healing can there be for the mother of a murdered son?

We lost a lovely, kind, and generous woman when Mrs McKinney died. In her death we can hope her grief has healed and she has found peace.

William Nash

Alex Nash and Bridget Doohey, the Boss and the Duchess, were married at 6.00 p.m., New Year's Eve 1942. Alex and Bridget had fourteen children. The first died at birth. Willie, Alex and Bridget's sixth son, was murdered by British Soldiers on 30 January, 1972. He was nineteen.

When Willie walked into a room, it wasn't so much his tussle of soft brown hair or his polished boots you noticed. His long lean frame, powerfully built, his hands, already callused from long days at men's labour, the smile that hinted at his mischievous nature, and his eyes, they just about made you melt. Willie was a dream.

His pictures don't reveal what an enormous presence he was, even at nineteen. His height hardly matched his long strong arms capped with the large rough hands of a man with docking in his blood. When he mounted the last stretch of road up to 38 Dunree Gardens at the end of a day's work, the children on the street ran up to him calling, 'Swing me around Tarzan!' And he did. The children squealed in delight as he scooped them up and spun them around.

The giggly one with the lopsided grin, Willie could melt your heart. But he was also a shit, he played so many pranks and practical jokes. At first, it was a boot or a shoe on top of the door. Willie left the door slightly ajar, and the minute you walked in the door, bang! Down came the boot and smacked you on the head. If you were clever enough to steal a kiss in the back garden, you could count on passions being cooled with a pan of water, compliments of Willie.

As he grew, so did the complexity of his pranks. For one of his favourites, he removed the light bulb, filled a pair of trousers with clothes, and waited. The unsuspecting victim mounted the stairs up to the second floor and the screams that followed were undeniable.

Willie had struck again. No matter how many times he did it, you never got used to the figure dropping down from the loft.

His genius was in his patience. The other children would help collect the bottles and tie them together with the long, clear string but they soon became bored lying in wait. Willie got the joy of pulling the bottles behind the unsuspecting passer-by. When the victim walked, the bottles followed along. Every time the walker stopped and looked, the bottles rested until, with one big tug, the bottles smashed and sent the victim darting into the night.

Willie's boldness earned him the pleasure of knick-knock, because before you got to watch the neighbours open the door to an empty porch, getting more upset each time, someone had to sneak up and tie the thread to the knocker. Willie's project management skills allowed him to enjoy the consternation caused when he executed the Mini-Cooper relocation plan, moving the car from the street down the way into the garden in front of a neighbour's house.

Though he's been gone a long time, you still half expect him to reach out and grab your leg as you pass by that shrub in the front of the house or his long arm to reach in the window and whack you with a stick as you watch TV.

In the spirit of, if you can't beat him, join him, the whole Nash family played jokes on each other and it continues to this day. Was the donkey in the bedroom a pint-sized attempt at a prank? Banty will have you believe it was just plain earnestness. That donkey's owner was really mean to the donkey. He loaded it down, drove it too hard, and was just a mean-spirited old coot who clearly did not have the donkey's best interests at heart. Six-year-old Banty led the rescue. Once the donkey was in the house, he managed to get it into his bedroom. But it just wouldn't hide under the bed when Banty heard his parents coming.

The prize for the most elaborate prank, however, goes to Bridget. When Alex turned sixty-five and applied for his pension, the office requested a birth certificate. In the days when Alex was born, recording births was not a high priority. A child was born at home and when someone got around to it, they went down to the office and recorded the birth. Family Bibles and baptismal certificates were a family's record of a birth, not a government-issued certificate.

To apply for the pension, Linda sent off for her father's birth certificate and received a stern letter asking if she were aware that giving

false information to the registrar was a serious offence. Linda knew exactly what her father knew – he was born 27 December 1919 on Blucher Street. She learned he was actually born on 28 June 1920 at 3 Howard Street. Alex, like the Queen of England, now had two birthdays – a real one and a celebratory one. When Alex learned the news, he thought it was a good thing because at Christmas he felt he was always done out 'cause his birthday presents and Christmas presents came together. Now he had 28 June. However, when he realised Father's Day was around this time, he needed to move his birthday to different date again.

The family speculated about the possible explanations for the misplaced birthday, but when Alex realised that his 28 June birthday made him a few months younger than Bridget, he realised he'd been had. Back then, you couldn't fall asleep because if you did, they'd pour water in your ears or paint you with soot from the fire. Nobody took naps during the day. Everyone tried to be the last one asleep at night. Today, you can't walk down the hall of a hotel with one

of them; they will knock on all the doors and dash off leaving you hanging as the rooms' occupants answer.

Some worked for a day, some for a season, but at one time or another, the Nash children all gathered spuds, earning their first shillings high in the green rolling hills of Derry. The children didn't wrestle with the irony of earning money for treats by picking potatoes in the same fields, and for the same aristocracy, that drove their ancestors from their country by their refusal to yield. They couldn't have known it would be the same stubborn refusal that would forever change their lives before they reached adulthood.

Like his friends and siblings, Willie left school at fifteen. Few Irish went on for higher education in Willie's generation. Unless you were going to be a priest, what was the point? Families needed to be housed, clothed, and fed. Work was work. You were lucky if you could get it, degree or not.

As children, they were trucked to the Waterside farms for work. Later they looked for anything that helped them contribute to the household. Girls went to work in the shirt factories, boys to whatever they could find, work in shops and pubs, the brewery, the quay. Some found their way to the training centre to learn a trade, such as painting, plumbing, or electric.

Willie went to work for Jackie Doherty's grocery on Central Drive. For two years he made deliveries on a bicycle with a basket on the front, his sister Maggie trailing after him. At seventeen, Willie joined his brothers, Da, and Granda down the quay.

The Nash men: Stiff, Tombstone, Banty, Allen, and Willie, three generations of Dockers, dressed in layers – shirt, jumper, jacket, and cap. It was their movement, more than anything, protecting them against the raw wind each day at sunrise. Keep moving. It keeps out the cold. Keep moving. It wards off hunger. Keep moving. There's a smoke and a few quid to be had down the quay.

The morning walk to the quay was two miles straight down. From Dunree Gardens, left onto Broadway, down the New Road, down Eastway by Essex Army Base, down Westland St, across Rossville St, up William St, through Waterloo Place, to Customs House Street. Head down; collar up. Morning was always fuckin' freezin'.

The Nashes worked for McKenzie's import/export business, which meant when the boats were waiting and the spuds delivered, they were guaranteed work. Twelve hours a day of eight stone bags from the lorry to the shed explains the massive upper bodies the Nash men still sport, even though the quay closed years ago.

The quay and the men who worked there are an essential part of Derry history, and the Nash family is part of the fabric of Irish families who made the Derry quay the most efficient docking system in Europe for generations. The quay was the only place where for years Irish men could find work and be rewarded for dedication and a job well-done as recognised by the button system. Here, they ran the show. The tradition of Derry dockers is of men so strong, it is hallowed in the lore of Dockers. The world the Derry dockers made was steeped in a pride of steadfast dedication to the job, strength, and efficiency that far outpaced even their fiercest competition in Belfast.

Half seven the men gathered for an 8 a.m. start. The Nashes reported to the Liverpool shed at the back of the Guildhall. Smoking cigarettes, doled out by the Duchess, they stamped their feet and chatted to ward off the damp cold wind. Dock work was a winter activity, but no matter the season, it's always cold down the quay. Granda Paddy (Stiff) worked the coal boats where a gang consisted of fourteen men and the gaffer who was employed to hire the men and collect dockets from the lorry drivers.

A steady-up man would guide and direct the winch operator. A bucket man sat on a platform which had a large bucket on it. When it was full, he pulled out a slip-pin which tilted the bucket and discharged the coal into a cart or lorry which had pulled up beside the platform. The remaining twelve men went into the hold when the hatches were lifted. They started to load the coal onto three one-ton buckets, four men to each bucket. On entering the hold, they stood on the coal and had to dig down through it with large, square-mouthed shovels to fill their buckets. As the discharge went on, the most welcome sight to the hold men was the floor of the boat because this meant the shovels could be pushed along the steel rather than down through the coal. These men were proud of their long-standing tradition of efficiency and endurance, and it is recorded that twelve men could discharge 120-150 tons of coal between the start of a boat at 8 a.m. and the 10 a.m. 'smokoe' or tea break. To put this into perspective, that is the equivalent of the twelve hold-men shovelling one ton of coal out of the hold every minute.[32]

For Alex (Tombstone), Willie, Banty, and Allen, work was on McKenzie's spud boats. The most labour intensive cargo of the lot, the potatoes arrived at the quay by lorry. Two planks were laid from the wharf to the boat. Two long ropes or slings were positioned at the bottom and two dockers (shore-men) would lift and place an eight-stone bag onto the shoulders of one of four men who carried ten such bags from the lorry to each sling. The sling was then tightened over the bags and secured onto the hook of the ship's winch which in turn deposited the sling load into the hold. Another four dockers (hold-men) then stowed the bags. The hold-men loaded the potatoes in such a way as to create steps so the bags could be carried to the top of the pile, efficiently filling the entire hold of the ship. As with other cargoes, a gaffer would hire the workforce, a steady-up man would direct the winch driver and a tally man kept count of all the bags going into the hold, giving a total of fifteen men to a gang. The men were proud of their reputation: Derry dockers took two and a half days to Belfast dockers' six to load the same tonnage.[33]

You could always tell the day by the dinner. Steak, pork chops, lamb chops, mince, sausages, and rissoles formed the foundation of the weekly meals. The pattern of which is recited with a tinge of nostalgia and gratitude that those days are past. Weekdays, after his dinner, Willie usually cat-napped in a chair for a bit and then was off to the club.

Saint Mary's Boys' Club was a converted barn at the top of Beechwood Avenue. One side of the barn had a boxing den, and the other side was a youth club with a coffee bar. At that time, 1965-7, St Mary's and Bishop's Field were the total amenities in Creggan. If you didn't attend the boys' club or play football, you basically went nowhere. A small club, it was frequented by an enormous crowd of young people and turned out its fair share of successful competitive boxers.

When they came of age, Willie and his friends were more often found at the pubs. The Rushes lived two doors down, Pat Ward and Tommy Hazelet rounded out the group that went out for the country music at the pubs down the town. Banty made friends with the Americans who learned soccer and in turn introduced them to basketball. Basketball never really caught on in Derry, but Americans and Irish have a common love of drinking and, God Bless America!, the soldiers had a line on a steady supply.

Alex took full advantage of his sons' early forays into Friday night drinking. Saturday mornings, the Nash sons slept soundly through measured commotion rising up from the kitchen, each movement carefully timed and taken so as not to rouse the Duchess. Alex knew where his sons had been each Friday and the condition of each on Saturday morning. Patrick and Edward had moved out. Joe and Michael were still school boys. But Alex was a lucky man, there were still the four in the one room, ripe for the picking.

First he shook Willie's shoulder, 'Wake up, son I've got a breakfast here – made it just for you.' Willie turned over, his long, lean frame stretched under the blanket, mop of brown hair showing signs of a deep sleep.

'It's early, go on Da'.

'Now look here son, the eggs are fresh, there's bacon and sausages, just the way you like 'em.'

Willie reached for his trousers, 'Here Da, if I give you a cupla bob will ya leave me be?'

'Aye Willie, that'll do.'

Next came Banty, 'Wake up son, I've got a breakfast here – made it just for you. Here let me get it down where you can smell it. Have a good sniff. Isn't that grand?'

'Aw, Da not again, hand me my trousers, there's a few bob in me front pocket.'

Alex shook Allen's shoulder. He kept his head under the army blanket. But a quid came out from under the covers, 'Here ya are, go on now.' By his pre-emptive strike, Allen avoided the nausea that washed over the others at the sight and smell of the full fry swimming in steaming lard.

Alex approached a waiting Charlie, upright in bed. As a non-drinker and boxer he was always the last to get the offer. On his way to becoming a seven-time all-Ireland national champion, he passed on the shakedown, relishing the grease-laden plate of eggs, sausage, black and white pudding, toast, and beans, preparing him for the training-day ahead.

Willie missed his brother's success. Willie's grave was still fresh as his family sent Charlie off to compete in the 1972 Olympic Games. He wasn't there when Charlie turned professional winning the Irish title, the British and Commonwealth title, and the European title, which he retired to fight for the world title. Keeping his collection complete, he came back to reclaim the European title.

After Alex's breakfast scam, Bridget took the rest of the boys' money on the Saturday night. The wage packets came on the Friday and just like her mother and mother-in-law before her, Bridie collected the money from her children and husband. Of the £4-5 the kids each earned, £3-4 went to the household and £1 to the worker. Bridie was the ruler of the roost and this included the distribution of cigarettes for the week: three fags in the morning, three for after lunch, one for the evening. The weekly dole of forty-nine cigarettes had to be paid for on the Friday. After the household contribution and the cigarette fee, the kids had about enough for a dance on the

Saturday night. But what Bridie didn't get from them for expenses and fags, they lost to her at cards. To say Bridie was a crack poker player is an understatement. You'd have a better chance playing against the devil, in which case you might have stood a chance at winning a hand or two. Bridie held court at the kitchen table, presiding over games that lasted through the wee hours of the morning.

You have to admire a woman who can raise thirteen children, manage a husband, and beat the pants off you in poker. She had her hands full with those boys. And Alex 'Tombstone' was the quietest man in Derry, until he got a drink in him. If you lived along the route Alex walked home, you'd probably heard 'Bicycle Built for Two' more than you wanted.

Alex belted the song out as he walked along Rossville Street to Westland, then up. Up Eastway by Essex Army Base, up the New Road, up Broadway and finally onto Dunree Gardens to the house. If he avoided the RUC in town and the army along Eastway Terrace, he'd come swinging in the door, 'What about you Duchess?' Boom! Bang! Over the head. 'Get up them stairs now!' and that was that. A good smack wasn't Bridget's only tool. A magic potion in his tea let him sleep for twenty-four hours after drink.

Like his peers, Alex was expected to turn over his unopened wage packet to his wife every week. There were necessary expenditures though – greyhounds, horse races, boxing matches, drink – for which Alex rightfully needed cash. The lengths he would go to get it and that Bridget would go to prevent his getting it were extraordinary.

The notes he hid in his sock were spirited out in the night and replaced with silver. His hidden trousers were recovered; the money concealed within liberated. Alex took to leaving extra gifts in his pockets. 'Always something there for the Duchess!'

Alex and Bridget Nash were in love. Rather then hugs or kisses, for Bridget and Alex it was a whack at the end of a night's drinking that was love. Their children never heard them utter the words, never saw it expressed, but they knew. They felt it. In the absence of pats, hugs, kisses, or words, it was there. A presence in the house no one could deny. Can you imagine feeling something so strong you never need to hear it? Knowing something so deep in your soul it never need be expressed externally? Could you spend the rest of your days secure in the love of your partner if he or she never again uttered the words? Alex and Bridget Nash, the Boss and the Duchess, they knew.

Willie never got the opportunity. No lucky girl ever got to be wrapped in his strong arms, run her fingers through his brown locks, lie next to him, her head on his chest on the cold Derry nights, watch him lift his children in the air and spin them around, tease him about his hair turning grey, bother him about the bills needing to be paid or the car needing repair.

When Willie was eighteen, he earned the right of passage that took many Derry lads from boyhood to manhood. He spent six months at Crumlin Road Jail.

The Select Bar stood facing Foyle Street, across from the present-day bus station. The three-story building held a shop on the ground floor and to the side a door that opened to stairs leading to the bar on floor two and the toilets on floor three. The space provided just enough room for a small bar, a few tables of four or five, and a three-piece band.

Eight friends out at the pub. There is probably not a single more ordinary happening in Derry. Banty, Allen, and Willie Nash, Paddy, Joe, and Noel Rush, Tommy Hazlet, and Pat Ward sat at a table on the second floor smoking and talking over a quiet pint. Danny Doran, alias George Washington, local country and western singer, was playing that night.

As the lads left the bar, they alighted down the one-body-wide staircase and encountered a police contingent. As the friends attempted to exit, an RUC arm came across and blocked the way out, 'Where the fuck you think youse are goin'?'

'We're leavin',' was Willie's reply. Banty didn't hear the details of the conversation, but he deduced that words were exchanged. No big deal, they were accustomed to verbal jibes from the RUC, but when the baton was raised above his head, Willie didn't flinch. He floored the cop. He wasn't out that day to be harassed and abused. One RUC man down, the friends scattered.

Unfortunately, Allen and Willie were lifted. Banty and Paddy watched helpless from the Derry walls as his brothers were loaded up and driven to Strand Barracks; Willie taking a baton beating in the back as they passed by. On 10 May 1971, Willie was sentenced to six months. He went to jail, served his time, and earned his 50 per cent remission. Due to be out in August, as Willie's release date drew near the RUC decided he'd been in an earlier brawl that deserved another six-month sentence. Without the benefit of trial, Willie was sentenced and served that six-month term as well, once again earning his remission. He was out of jail just two months before he was murdered.

On 26 January 1972 Bridget had a heart attack. She was in hospital when Willie was murdered, waked, and buried. She never got to stroke her dead son's hair, gaze on his face in his casket, kiss him goodbye. Bridget didn't get to escort her murdered son to his grave. Instead, Bridget was locked away in a hospital room, helpless, unable to take his last steps with him just as she had been present when he took his first.

Was her heart weak from the physical strain of an attack, or was her heart broken grieving for her murdered son that took Bridie just seven years later? Her family knew a woman who never recovered from the news her son was murdered, waked, and buried while she lay in hospital helpless to care for him, to be with him, to say goodbye as he left the world.

The bullet that ripped through Willie's heart seemed to tear her heart as well, but Bridget never spoke of her own grief. 'Saw poor Mrs Kelly down the town today, she's suffering so, yer heart just breaks for her.' Bridget wasn't the same woman after Willie's death. She stopped visiting her children. She was completely shattered. Her family watched helplessly as she struggled to mend her wounded heart, as she was diagnosed with diabetes, as she ached for the other mothers of dead sons. She was buried with her Willie on 19 May 1979.

Bridget suffered the fate of other Derry mothers of murdered sons. Alex was afforded an opportunity denied the other Derry men whose sons were murdered on Bloody Sunday. Alex was there. He was close enough to shout out, to race to Willie's side. But before Alex could call his name, a bullet entered Willie's right chest cavity, passed through the upper part of his right lung, through his right atrium, his heart sac, abdominal cavity, and diaphragm. It lacerated his inferior vena cava, lacerated his liver, his right suprarenal gland and right kidney then exited through the right side of his back. Before the sound of his father's voice reached him, Willie lay dying on the Rossville Street rubble barricade.

Alex raced to his son's side. He raised his hands over his head in an attempt to stop the shooting. For his heroism, for the love of his son, Alex was rewarded with two gunshot wounds. He was rewarded with the sight of his son being tossed like an animal into the back of a Saracen. Lifted by the hands and feet, Willie was tossed in with the bodies of Michael McDaid and John Young, who were also taken from the rubble barricade and contaminated by the poisonous hands of British soldiers, filthy with gunshot residue.

Alex Nash changed after Bloody Sunday. He blamed himself for Willie's death. A father is supposed to protect his sons. A father is supposed to die before his sons. Alex stepped into to a hail of bullets but he couldn't turn back time. The bullet that ripped though Willie's heart, through Bridget's heart, tore Alex's open as well. He often said, 'You should never bury a son or a daughter, they should bury you. It's not the natural way of things.'

Alex suffered. For years he had travelled to England to paint in the summers, earning much-needed cash. Money that fed and clothed his family. After Willie was murdered, Alex never returned to England. Alex seemed desperately to want to die. He taunted the soldiers and the RUC so relentlessly they crossed the street to avoid him. The British Army raided the Nash home just as relentlessly, gathering the family into the small sitting room at the front, and then ransacking the house. But they never entered the room where Alex slept.

Did he believe he should have died too? Was he haunted by the sight of his son's murder? Was he tortured by the fact that he could not stop it? Was Alex further destroyed because he couldn't protect his family from the hate mail, telling them their son deserved to die; the British press that excoriated the men and boys killed, calling them terrorists; and the constant pursuit by the British Army that terrorised his children and particularly his daughters?

Years after the Duchess was buried, Alex was still talking about her as if she were just out in the kitchen. She was always there with him. The night Alex died, the night he was finally granted the gift to be with his wife and son, he was peaceful and serene. At that moment, Banty learned that the best measure of a life is the love you leave when you're gone; that what counts is how you care for and look after your family.

Some people are important to a community because they are political leaders, businessmen, or activists. The Nashes are important to Derry because they are part of the fabric of the place. The Nash family is a part of the history and traditions of Derry because they embody nearly every Derry tradition handed down. So much so that to say Nash Family Tradition is nearly the same as to say Derry City Tradition. Humour, docking, family, motherhood, church, walking, employment and lack thereof, housing and lack thereof, smoking, quitting smoking, drinking, quitting drinking, and story telling are all part of what makes the Nashes a family and Derry a city.

A grab on and don't let go, full throttle, don't do anything small kind of family, that's the Nashes. Alex, Bridget, Willie, and his twelve brothers and sisters are not the biggest family in Derry, but they manage to be one of the best known. It could be their history as Dockers, their three generations of boxers, or just their live-out-loud approach to life.

When we come to understand the tragedy of Willie's death, the injustice of it, and the pain it caused, we release the truth hidden in the moral rubble of Bloody Sunday. And the truth, eventually, will set the Nash family – and countless others – free.

Michael McDaid

Michael was the second youngest of our family of twelve. At the time of his death he had seven brothers and four sisters. Michael was twenty years and four months old when a British soldier ended his beautiful life, and put a bright light out in my family.[34]

An old machine washed two bottles at a time but Michael preferred to do it by hand. The whole operation was set up in the wrong direction. The optic measure attached from right to left. The brass rod threaded through the siphons from right to left. Michael was left handed. He adapted. He bottled three barrels of Guinness a week. At fifty-dozen bottles a barrel, Michael washed, dried, filled, and tended 1,800 bottles every week.

Monday he washed the bottles. Tuesday they dried. Wednesday morning the delivery arrived. The three barrels of Guinness in place, corked and waiting, Michael set up the bottling machine. Bend over; lift four bottles; dispense beer; cork bottles using foot pump; place bottles in crate to brew for two weeks. Repeat 450 times. Monotonous, hard work, dedicated attention to detail, customers to tend to in the bar, week in, week out. Michael loved it.

The day-patrons – retired teachers, milkmen, postmen, accountants, factory workers, coalmen, dockers, and the unemployed – supervised operations while perched on crates set in a half-circle around the bottling line. Lengthy discussions on international politics to the rhythm of the process were the order of the weekdays.

Thursday and Friday the bottles rested. The crowd picked up. Danny Doherty used a crutch and always sat at the table to the left of the bottling process. Jim McBride, 'Hambone,' who worked with horses and was a big strong man with a great toothy smile, joked with all the customers. The sheepskin curer turned out some fine skins but look at him crossways and he mighta said – What are you looking at? The two men engaged in conversation between the glass divides were oblivious to the others.

Bang! Michael slammed the bottle of stout on the bar, 'There ya go, Leo, drink up!' Leo Carlin lived behind the Brandywell, the football pitch just across from Bradley's. Displaced from his local through redevelopment, Leo started drinking in Bradley's just before Michael came over from the shop. They became fast friends. 'Michael worked every Friday night. He served forty or fifty patrons and knew them all by name. He knew their personalities and how to wind them up, but they all loved him. Michael was a great man for pranks, especially on the older men. He liked to keep them laughing. Mickey would get Danny talking to somebody and then lift the crutch and hide it'.[35]

The bar was 'The Celtic' but everybody called it Bradley's. The family owned it and the attached grocery for three generations. Tall and gray, Bradley's stood at the corner of Elmwood Road and Stanley's Walk. If you entered the corner door for the grocery, you found four hundred square feet of spuds, turnips, beetroot, bread, sugar, flour, tea, everything required for the family larder. Order at the front of the shop, and it was sent out by delivery.

Upon exiting the grocery, a left turn onto Elmwood Road took you to the bar. The first door was the snug. A wee place where maybe a man and his wife would have a bottle or a wee drink on the quiet. The snug kept secrets. Like men who enjoyed the company of their wives and sons who didn't want their fathers to know they drank.

The second door opened onto the bar. A man's bar. Guinness bottling to the right, bar to the left. A few tables seating three or four each dotted the back wall. The bar was divided by panes of glass, four or five at two-foot intervals which allowed the patrons to enjoy a quiet drink and conversation.

Bradley's was a quiet bar during the week but come the weekend, Mickey's forty or fifty drank and sang. According to John Bradley, 'some of them had been professional singers so they sang songs and had a tremendous time. At that time money was not plentiful, so they drank a little and sang a lot. It was a friendly place and very much because Michael was part of the whole. The Celtic was a place where everybody had a very enjoyable time and he took part in the fun.'

The Bradley family had operated the grocery and bar for three generations when Michael joined the staff. In the two and a half years he stocked and delivered, he became part of the family. When Mickey started at Bradleys, he worked as a messenger boy for the shop. Delivering the spuds, turnips, beetroot, bread, sugar, flour, and tea, Mickey got on very well with all the customers, especially the older ones. He always made sure they had everything they required. Nothing was too much to ask of him.

John Bradley recalls:

> Michael worked very hard. He was a unique young man in the sense of his age group. I was a contemporary of his. I lived and was reared only two hundred yards away so I'd known him since his childhood, and he had a very respectable family. The reason I say he was unique is because he dressed in a manner uncharacteristic of young people in the sense that he wore a collar, tie, and a sports coat. His trousers were immaculately ironed. Never was a crease in them. His shoes were always shined. He was this way when first he came to work for us at sixteen. He was very different from the other young men running around at that time. He was respectable, quiet spoken, and a hard-working industrious young man as well.

In the autumn of 1968, the Bradleys' long-time barman got an offer to join DuPont, a good job with great pay and benefits. For Derry men such jobs were a long time coming, so when offers from DuPont finally came, they took them. It was a hard blow to the Bradley family who had depended on him for a decade. Mr Bradley, getting past the age of long hours and bottling Guinness, looked to his manager to take over. The family was devastated.

John Bradley, just off to university, decided to abandon his plans to become an accountant and return home to take over the bar when his father had a brilliant idea. Why not Mickey? He'd been at the shop for two years. In that time he had worked hard and been an asset to the business. Lately he'd been helping out more frequently at the bar. He didn't smoke or drink. He was always well dressed and polite. Everyone liked him. He loved his work. Why not let Mickey have a go at managing the bar?

It wasn't long before the Bradley's realised they had struck gold. They'd had the perfect match with them for the last two years and Mickey found the perfect job – this was what he was supposed to do. Bradley's bar and the Bradley family soon became Mickey's second home and family. Before long, the elder John Bradley was grooming Mickey as he planned to groom his own son to run the bar. No doubt Bradley's Bar would be Michael's some day.

According to Leo, 'Mr Bradley put a lot of trust and faith in Michael and Michael was loyal to Mr Bradley. He never let him be interrupted. Michael handled the daily business of the bar and took over the bottling process as well. In fact, Mickey would've been one of the last of the young people to bottle Guinness.'

Michael's work ethic and enthusiasm for the bar and patrons was very important to John, who went on to become a successful accountant. 'I remember very well my father writing to me and saying Michael McDaid had been doing a very good job in the grocery shop and had graduated essentially into the bar and was doing a few evenings work in the bar. He had proven to be a fantastic worker, very popular with the customers. There needed to be no question of my giving up a university career. That was very significant to me. I was always grateful to Michael for that.'

At the close of business Saturday, Michael closed out the tabs, bid goodnight to the few still lingering, washed the glasses, wiped the bar's mahogany finish to a deep glow, shined it's glass divides, stood at the door, and surveyed his work. Someday he would be the proprietor. He was being groomed for the role. It fit him like a glove.

Michael turned off the lights, locked the door and left. He walked one hundred yards along Elmwood, then left for number 22. Click. Click. Click. The sound reassured his mother. Her Mickey was coming up the street, his iron-tipped heel ticking on the concrete footpath. Now she could sleep.

If the staccato of the bottling process and the repetitive nature of the bar business was the rhythm of Mickey's life, his mother, Cathleen, supplied the melody. Michael's mother infused joy into her family. Every morning, 4.30 a.m. saw Mickey's mother in the kitchen making dough. As it rose, so did her children. Twelve, all told, up for school or work, washed, dressed, fed, and out. By 7.00 a.m. she was cutting the gravy rings and doughnuts. Sent with one of the boys to the shops in town on the weekdays; lined in boxes for the morning queue outside her door on the Sunday. Scones, apple cakes, gravy rings, wedding cakes, Cathleen's kitchen and front room supported a cottage industry.

Pre-dawn to dark of night she worked. She hummed. She sang. She never complained. She lived a Derry mother's life: she loved her children, was dignified, strong, and happy. She created a place to which her children always returned. When the McDaid children left home, they didn't scatter to the wind. Beechwood Street, Stanley's Walk, and Marlborough Road are all a stone's throw from the family home in Tyrconnell Street. Some went to England for work, but the McDaid family was always in touch, and Cathleen's children landed home regularly.

In 1970 Michael and Cathleen bought a dark-green Ford Cortina. The 1600 cc, four-door with radio was Michael's pride and joy. He kept it immaculate and it changed his family's life. Before the car, a day-trip to the beach was a huge operation. It meant planning, packing, and riding the bus forty-five minutes each way. After the car, it was just a matter of jumping into the car and away they went. Before the car, a day-trip to Buncrana was the extent of the family holiday, a trip to Galway or a night's stay was out of the question. This suited Michael's father, John, as he preferred to sleep at home, in his own bed. But that fact didn't necessarily stop the rest of the family. The car meant Mickey and his mother could scheme a weekend holiday. As Michael's younger brother Kevin remembers it:

> Mickey and our mother must have cooked up the plan, because when we loaded into the car that morning my father and I didn't know the boot was packed. We headed toward Bundoran, about an hour and a half down the road. We stopped for tea and sandwiches and it was still early so Mickey says, 'Why don't we just go on a bit further?'
>
> Well, it ended up we arrived in Galway about eight thirty or nine that night. My father ranted and raved – 'you planned this!' Ordinarily we could ply him with a stout or a whiskey, but not this night. We really did ourselves in. We booked into a caravan park for the night and were going to go into town to hear some music but if Dad wasn't having any fun – nobody was having fun so we were sent for take-away and ate chicken, fish, and chips in the park.

Galway is the gateway to Connemara National Park, Corrib County, and the rugged, beautiful Aran Islands. The city is filled with shops, pubs, restaurants, museums, and galleries. The Salthill suburb of Galway boasts fairground attractions and sandy beaches for swimming, sunning, and fishing. At the time of their trip, the weather was brilliant, sunny and warm, perfect for a few days' sightseeing but the McDaids saw none of it. They set out for home as soon as the sun rose the next morning.

Kevin recalls:

> It was an adventure for me. I was only sixteen then and it was great to
> get in the car like we never had a worry. Galway was over the border,
> just 175 miles, but it was really the other side of the world for us. It
> might look like it turned out to be just a drive but it was an amazing
> trip. We had a lot of laughs. I enjoyed it from minute we left till we
> got back. Me and Mickey had a great laugh that night. Our father
> was a good character and we enjoyed the craic.

Before the car, most Sundays passed uneventfully. After the car, most
Sundays Michael took his mother, sister Bridie and her boys, Seamus,
Hugo, and Damian to the beach. Bridie's house sits on Beechwood
Street, smack between Bradley's and the family home. From Bradley's,
Mickey watched for his nephew Seamus walking to and from the
Long Tower School. He thoroughly enjoyed the boys and called in

daily to play with his nephews. He got Seamus to take his first steps and say his first words. 'See you later', Michael called. 'See you later!' Young Seamus called back.

In the summer of 1971 Cathleen rented a Buncrana beach house for the month of June. Bridie and her sisters took their youngsters out of school and went off to the beach. Mickey landed down on his nights off; husbands and brothers at the weekends. It was a brilliant month. The weather was great. Just a half hour walk to the beach, the three-bedroom concrete bungalow had an old range – in the mornings, the women prepared the dinner and left it in the stove. The stew or steak, gravy, and spuds were ready when they returned in the afternoon. Then, back to the beach in the evening.

Bridie's boys had just received their first boxing gloves and part of the craic at night was their first attempt at Derry's most popular sport. The house was just outside Buncrana next to a farm and the children had hours of fun chasing chickens and 'tending' the other animals. Filled with a lot of play, some drinking, a whole raft of singing, laughter, and much joy, it was the last summer holiday they would share with Michael.

No one knew that beginning at 8.16 p.m. on 30 January 1971, the year preceding Michael's murder, every day with him, every memory of him, would be the last.

Memories like the tape recorder. Bridie recalls when Michael won it at a rickety wheel a few weeks before Christmas 1971. He brought it to her house, sneaked up the stairs and taped the boys chattering before they went to sleep. The tape recorder went back and forth between Bridie and her mother's house with messages for a bit of craic. The McDaid family song – a well-kept secret – is stored on one remaining tape, one with Mickey's precious voice and laughter.

Memories like Christmas, 1971. As always, after midnight Mass, the family landed at Cathleen's for a fry and some time together – women in the kitchen, men in the living room – they chatted and joked until half two or so in the morning and then carried tired children home to bed and parents' final preparations for Christmas morning.

That Christmas morning Michael and his parents arrived early at Bridie's. Bridie and her husband Hugo gave their boys a large Lego set, and over the next few weeks Michael spent hours building cars and castles with the boys.

The next Wednesday Mickey collected his mother Bridie and his nephews Hugo, Damian, and Seamus. The merry band drove off to Strabane, Cathleen's birth place. They visited her family home, school, and parents' family homes. Cathleen told lovely stories of her school days, and of old friends. It was a wonderful afternoon.

The morning of 30 January 1972, Bridie and Hugo met Michael at Tyrconnell Lane. He was on his way to Creggan, where he was meeting Leo Carlin, Paddy Doherty, and Eamonn McLaughlin for the start of the march. They were jubilant. They were going to see the biggest crowd that had attended a march. They spent a few minutes talking, said good-bye, and parted ways. It was the last time Bridie saw her brother alive.

The day, and life as they knew it, ended for the McDaid family at about half eight. It was natural for the family to gather at their home on Tyrconnell, and they did. They gathered and waited. Rumours spread that Mickey had been arrested. His family was not officially informed that he was dead until the evening. A pall set upon the house. The click of Mickey's heel on the street letting Cathleen know her son was home safely was silenced.

Michael's family was devastated. His mother was never the same. No one in the family ever heard her hum or sing a tune again. His sister remembers him as 'a fine, decent, honest, hard-working, loving, human being. He had so much to offer, yet he was gunned down. My family was not the only one robbed by his death. The people of Derry were robbed also. They were robbed of a special person, someone who cared for others more than himself, someone who could have made a difference.' Her sentiments are echoed in the words of Michael's friends.

Leo Carlin was traumatised by the events of Bloody Sunday. He was shot at, marched with a rifle to his face and arrested. He lost two close friends, Mickey and Paddy Doherty. He still grieves deeply for the McDaid and Doherty families' loss, and reflects:

> He was only twenty. Michael was only twenty when he was killed. Michael was a great lad. His whole family, his mother and father were brilliant people. When I gave my statement to the Inquiry it was terrible hard to do because I never spoke to anybody about Bloody Sunday. In fact you're the first stranger I've ever talked to about Bloody Sunday. I never spoke to my wife about it. Michael was along with me that day he was shot. We were together he, and I, and Paddy Doherty. They were both killed.

John Bradley says:

> Michael was very popular with the customers and his death was a terrible loss to everybody. Michael left his mark on all the various people that came into the bar and his death left a terrible void. My father, who died in 1973, was a father figure in totality. When anyone was in crisis, he was the man to come to. He was very respectable and would have been regarded as a pillar of society. He regarded Michael as one of the family; as a very important member of our family, and so, we all got very close to him. His death at such a young age was such a terrible loss. As a family we take Michael's murder very much to heart and it still affects us.

Michael's brutal murder by callous, indifferent soldiers stands in stark contrast to his warm and kind humanity. By any criteria Michael McDaid was the opposite of a Derry Young Hooligan. Like thousands of others he joined the march as witness to the injustices heaped upon Derry Irish. He was no different than the countless Americans who marched in civil-rights demonstrations. He was no different than his neighbours who were clean of the IRA but clear in their intent to send a message: 'Internment is wrong.'

Michael's intent was to attend the march, meet his girlfriend, go home, have his dinner, and go to bed. The next day he would return to Bradley's to do his work and resume conversations with his friends and customers. Michael died as an innocent and his death touched the hearts of family and loved ones in a profound way.

Thinking about Mickey one afternoon, Bridie sat down and wrote about her brother. Her words conclude:

> The last time I saw Michael alive was shortly before the march on Bloody Sunday. My husband and I were taking our sons to my mother's house, she was minding them, as Hugo and I were going to the march. It would be my first ever march. We met Michael at Tyrconnell Lane. He was on his way to Creggan for the start of the march. He was like myself and everyone else in Derry that day – jubilant, we were going to see the biggest crowd that had ever been at a march before. We spent a few minutes talking, then we said good-bye. Little did I know that the next time I would see Michael, he would be in a coffin!
>
> Twenty-six years on, my brother Michael is still held in high regard, and spoken of frequently by those who knew him. This speaks volumes for the type of person he was, and encapsulates fully the essence of why his death was so very wrong.

Michael's memory shines bright, vibrant and everlasting. It will be passed from generation to generation with love.

Paddy Doherty

Paddy just loved his children. He was a very simple man. He never wanted anything. He lived for us and that was it.[36]

Three months after her eleventh birthday, Karen Doherty became a fatherless daughter. Karen's dad died when he went off to walk in a civil-rights march one day. She loved her father with all her heart.

After her father's death, Karen became largely responsible for her five younger siblings. Karen was her father's daughter – stubborn, proud, passionate. But she didn't know how to be a fatherless daughter. Paddy taught his daughter to tie her shoes, cook the meals, and mind her brothers and sisters. He never taught her how to live without him.

Paddy Doherty was thirty-one years old when he was killed. He had been a husband and father for eleven years, his wife, Eileen, giving birth to six children. They had the first four in four years, a five-year break, and then two more. They were all born at the start and the finish of the month: Karen the 31 October; Patrick the 27 November; Tony the 1 January; Paul the 1 February; Colleen the 28 February; and Gleann the 2 June, so it might be said that the happiest days for Paddy were at the start and the end of the month!

Eileen's mother proposed. She called Paddy in and said, 'It's done. You'll be getting married now.' The dress was pink satin with three-quarter-length sleeves and a full skirt. Pink veil, white gloves, and white shoes completed the ensemble. Paddy, the handsomest man in Derry, was dashing in his navy single-breasted suit. She had to kneel outside the altar but she was marrying the man she'd loved for two and a half years. He smiled, held her hands in his, recited his vows, and kissed her. Everything was right with the world.

On Easter Tuesday at 8 a.m. the wedding Mass was followed by a fry for a hundred guests at the house at the top of Central Drive. While the guests stayed on to toast the couple, Paddy and Eileen departed for their honeymoon. Eighteen years of age. The eldest of thirteen. Her first time away from home. Tears fell as Eileen waved goodbye to her father on the platform. She and Paddy were too young to be getting married. Too young to be parents. But it was done. They were in love. They would do the best they could. Six months later, Karen arrived and Paddy took to parenting like a duck to water. He loved his daughter with all his heart.

Karen knew her father for only eleven years. She had all of those wonderful 'being in awe of your dad' years. The time in life when your father can do no wrong. The time when his punishments are justified, his expectations reachable, and his praise lavish. A time when a girl's desire to please her father is rewarded.

Karen was first born. A place of privilege in her father's eyes. Long walks by the River Foyle after her siblings were put to bed was a

special treat. Working by her father's side in the kitchen while he prepared the Sunday dinner made her feel grown-up. Placing her small hand in his large one when they walked to Mass and then standing at the back of the chapel with her father and the other men solidified for her the fact that she was Paddy Doherty's daughter. Paddy Doherty – strong, hard working, respected in the community, liked by his peers, and loved by his family – she was his daughter.

Paddy wasn't just Karen's best friend, confidant, and role model, he was her protector. He punished her brothers when they wronged her. When she returned from school one day to find her prized possession, an Elvis poster the size of her bedroom wall, suffering an injury of graffiti at the hand of a brother, Paddy lined up the three potential suspects, Tony, Paul, and Patrick and interrogated them like a New York City detective on a bad day. The fact that the poster was a gift from Paddy to Karen didn't help the boys' case.

When a drunk neighbour stumbled into Karen's room one night, Paddy went to the man's house, knocked on the door, said, 'Excuse me Madame, I'm real sorry to have to do this,' took the man outside, and taught him some manners, Karen knew he would always defend her honour.

Paddy was a Renaissance man. The father of a new generation. His house was one of equality. He and Eileen both worked and everyone in the house was expected to contribute a fair share. For the children this meant everyone had chores – boys and girls alike hoovered, scrubbed, and cooked.

This was a dramatic departure from the way Paddy and Eileen's generation had been raised. They were treading unchartered child-rearing waters, but their children didn't know that. The boys knew they were hoovering, cooking, washing dishes, and cleaning the yard while their friends were playing football. They knew that other girls were kept in while Karen went out for late-night walks with her dad. In the Doherty house it was age and family-contribution, not gender that earned you perks.

In retrospect, the Doherty siblings think that Paddy was concerned about making sure his family was brought up as properly and decently as possible, and that he wanted his children to be productive members of their community. Paddy was aware of social justice. He wanted his children to have the same rights and privileges as their Protestant peers. It certainly wasn't going to be anything they did that brought on governmental mistreatment. Paddy was raising his children to be equal members of what he hoped would become a just society.

To this end the children got paid sixpence every Friday night. They all contributed and they were all rewarded. They also attended Mass every morning. Every week-day morning they rose at six, dressed, and were sent up the hill to Long Tower Chapel. They went to Mass, trudged back home for breakfast, then back over the same route to school. Paddy worked to ensure there would be no spoiled children in the Doherty household.

Even so, Paddy seemed to know each of his children's special desires and he particularly indulged their wishes on their birthday: a big red bus for a very small Paul; a secret camera for Patrick for whom Paddy lined up all the other children in the backyard for a photo that turned out to be a hosing of water and a host of laughter from Paddy and Patrick; a bike for Tony.

Paddy made them each feel as if he knew them. He made a connection with his children as individuals. Colleen can't remember it but it was she that spent the most time snuggled in her father's arms and sitting in his lap. It was she that brought him home from the pub so Paddy spent more evenings helping with homework, wrestling, and laughing with his children than he did drinking with his friends.

Paddy was a family man. But he didn't just spend time with his wife and children. He got on great with Eileen's parents, too. Mrs Quigley set high expectations, telling Paddy in no uncertain terms how she expected him to treat her daughter and grandchildren, but she doted on him as well. Eileen's father was a traditional Derry man. He worked. He drank. He gambled. As different as Paddy was in that respect, Eileen's father had a great affinity with Paddy as a man's man.

Eileen's parents and her twelve siblings lived on Central Drive. A favourite destination of the Doherty children, they had no idea how

intimately acquainted they were fated to become with the household. In contrast to the Doherty's, a white-glove house of order, the Quigley house was a whirlwind of activity. Packed full of teenagers, the house reverberated with The Beatles, Rolling Stones, and The Kinks. Mrs Quigley was an avid baker and the house always smelled of bread and buns.

The Quigley's was also the place for parties. Christmas especially, when the lorry pulled up to deliver beer and lemonade; Sinatra crooned from the record player; stories were exchanged; and towards the end of the evening, men sang to their wives. Except in Paddy's case, his wife sang to him. Eileen was a great singer and was always prompted by her father to sing for the crowd. After all, Eileen was her father's daughter.

Paddy's desire to raise his children well: to be productive members of society, respect their neighbours, and participate meaningfully in their religion was reflected in his civil-rights activities. Not only did he want his children to be good people, he wanted them to live in a fair and just society. Just like fathers of black children in the Southern United States, Paddy took to the streets to make his desires known.

His children were only vaguely aware of Paddy's participation in civil-rights marches and his contribution of strength and determination in the Battle of the Bogside, when Eileen and the children evacuated to Central Drive for protection and waited anxiously for Paddy's return. After three solid days of defending the Bogside, Paddy was safely home. His hands and face pure black, he emerged from the Bogside walking up Westway to Creggan. Exhausted, he went inside, ate, went straight to bed, and didn't get up until the next morning.

On 30 January 1972, Paddy joined Leo Carlin, Michael McDaid, and Eamonn McLaughlin on the Civil Rights March against internment. They were a good way back in the crowd and reached Barrier 14 as the crowd began dispersing. They didn't know why the crowd was running away from the barrier but they joined them and took off down Chamberlain Street. Here Leo split off from his friends.[37]

When Soldier F gunned Paddy down he didn't know he was a family man. He didn't know that six young children would be fatherless. Soldier F was a paratrooper; a soldier trained to do a job. He was given orders, which he executed. After all, if he violated orders by killing Paddy, his commander certainly wouldn't have been decorated by the Queen.

The army thought Soldier F was a good soldier. They say the paratroopers are the best of the best in the British military. What kind of soldier shoots an unarmed man in the back?

Doherty had been shot between the rear of Block 2 of Rossville Flats and Joseph Place while crawling along the ground with a handkerchief held over his face. He had been hit from behind by a bullet which entered his buttock and proceeded through his body almost parallel to his spine. Lord Widgery found that he had not been carrying a weapon when he was shot.[38]

It wasn't Soldier F's job to know Paddy was a family man or to know he had six small children at home. It was Soldier F's job to execute an operation according to orders, not to concern himself with the fact that that his actions would lead to the devastation of a family.

This soldier's actions left Karen Doherty fatherless. He left a young girl with no strong arms to protect her. No shoulder to cry upon.

No man to confide in. No more Sunday dinners to prepare. No walks by the River Foyle. No father to walk her down the aisle. No grandfather to greet her newborn children. Though Soldier F took Karen's first love on a clear day in January, he did not darken the light within her, because Karen will always be Paddy Doherty's daughter.

Jackie Duddy

My sisters Maureen, Bernie, and Kay loved Jackie. They'd say, 'He was so sweet and placid. He was always smiling. You could never rile him. He was so good to the young ones. He had a lovely nature.' Well, he punched me up in the front hall and made me carry his boxing gear to the gym and back every night and that was one hell of a walk! He was nothing special, just my older brother.[39]

My name is Michael Duddy. I was born on 21 October 1960. My dad wrote a note to get Kay out of school to watch the little ones, 'Please excuse Kay from school as we have been blessed with another gift from God.' I was the fourteenth. Kay's school teachers were amazed at how the letter was worded – that it was still considered a gift from God even though it was the fourteenth. Pauline arrived three years and ten days after me, and she's the baby, so there's just the fifteen of us. Well, fourteen now, since Jackie's dead.

My brother Jackie was born on 7 July 1954. That was when my family still lived in Springtown Camp. My mother loved Springtown. There are stories of water running down the walls and disease and children dying, but my parents were one of the first to move their family into the huts so at that time they were still in good condition. They were damp and there was no central heating or bathroom. Maureen and Bernie and Kay remember the tin bucket where they bathed in front of the fire. Considering the condition of the houses in town at that time, this was definitely an upgrade.

Ma used to say she wished they had knocked her hut down and built a house there 'cause there was big rooms and lots of land around. But for the children, moving to Creggan Heights was like moving into a three-bedroom mansion because it was a brand new house with a bathroom, hot and cold running water, a fire, and a big back garden.

Everyone called Gerry, Patrick, and Jackie the three musketeers. Jackie and Patrick were a year and twenty days apart. Gerry came along another eighteen months later but he was the biggest of the three so a lot of people referred to Gerry, Patrick, and Jackie when it was actually Jackie, Patrick, and Gerry. Nonetheless, they looked near enough alike to be triplets.

When Gerry was born we outgrew the kitchen and started eating in shifts. At Christmas we set up a table in the sitting room so we could all eat while the food was hot, otherwise the wains were fed first, then the school-age group, and the ones out working would eat their dinner when they got in after work.

The bread man delivered maybe eight or ten loaves a day. On the bank holiday, when the bread man couldn't come for two or three days, there was something like twenty-four or thirty-six loaves delivered to our house, because no matter what you ate you had bread along with it to try and fill you. At least two loaves of bread always sat on the table at any dinner regardless of what the dinner happened to be. The bread was the filling bit. There might not have been much meat or spuds in the stew but there was gravy and you dipped your bread into it and got your fill. We always had friends in, especially the boys, and there was always enough so they got their share as well.

Each week the girls were given this wee note and they went down to the shop and left it off for the delivery man. The note would have listed maybe six pounds of butter, six pounds of jam, and twenty pounds of spuds, peas, fish, roast, chicken, and cabbage. The dinners were set for each week and there wasn't any such thing as two or three dinners being made to satisfy the fussy ones. You ate it or left it and if you didn't eat it you would have plenty of bread and jam to fill you up. Funnily enough, Gerry was the fittest and he was the one who lived mostly on the bread and jam.

Saturdays Jackie and his pals went to the pictures. Jackie liked the Westerns. There was a time when all these European film production companies made Westerns. They made something like six hundred of them between 1960 and 1975. The critics hated the films and because most of them were financed by Italian companies, they called them

Spaghetti Westerns. Jackie not only liked the films but he bought the records and listened to the scores over and over again! His favourites were all Clint Eastwood films: *A Fistful of Dollars*, *A Few Dollars More*, and *The Good the Bad and the Ugly*. He loved how Clint always 'rode into town'.

When Jackie was twelve he started boxing at the Long Tower Boxing Club. There was a boxing bill every week, Creggan one week, then Long Tower, St Mary's, St Eugene's, Strabane, etc. In only four years he'd won hundreds of trophies. There were two sports in Derry at the time, boxing and football. Our family did more boxing. Gerry started after Jackie but trained at St Mary's and as soon I came up, I joined the club as well.

Long Tower Club was a converted terrace house on Alexander Place just off Foyle Road. After dinner we left the house and walked down Bligh's Lane, down Stanley's Walk, up over the fly-over, down Bishop Street, before turning left into Alexander Place. We lived at

the top of Derry and the Long Tower Club was at the bottom just before the river.

In between the workout of walking to the club and back home, we got warmed up with jacks, sit-ups, lunges, and skipping. Then we broke up into speed bag, heavy bag, and sparring. You did so many exercises and then the groups switched around. Depending on the night, you could get some rest awaiting your turn.

The only heating was this old fire and that was only when the club was open. Nights when Jackie had a fight coming up and the club wasn't open, he would need a sparing partner. This meant Muggings (Gerry) had to go down with him and then get the head punched off him in the cold just so Jackie would be prepared for the fight. Jackie dragged us down to that club in all types of weather – from the top of Creggan down to Alexander Place and then back up again.

I got my first boxing lessons in the hallway in Central Drive. In the short, narrow hallway Jackie could get us up against the front door or against the stairs and use us as his punching bag. There were six boys and it seems like he practiced on all of us. Jackie was our first sparing partner and eventually we all took a turn at boxing, but Jackie was the only one who went anywhere with it.

Jackie trained to win. He boxed to win. It's what kept him going. At the time, to work so hard that your body is exhausted, your arms hang at your sides, until you are battered and weak, and all for the possibility of winning one match, seemed a little over the top to me. But to be the best was Jackie's driving force. Winning was the thing that motivated him to keep going. He became obsessed. It was his first and only love in life. For a while, everything took a backseat to boxing. But by being obsessed he was successful. If you are obsessed about other things – a girl, the drink, a job – they might lock you up. If you are obsessed about a sport, you are a hero.

At only fifteen years of age he went down to Dublin to compete in the All-Ireland Championship. He got beat in the finals. The people he boxed with all went on to become champions so he was in a good class of fighters. Dad loved it – him bringing in his trophies. He was so proud of Jackie's boxing.

Me da always said he was an ambassador for Ireland. He was in the Merchant Navy for a time and he said this was his role in life – to be in the Merchant Navy, travel the world, and be an ambassador for Ireland. He told us it was very important no matter what we done or where we went to always uphold this ideal that we were ambassadors. He always said he was a cosmopolitan. Later, when the army came in, he was like, 'Why are youse raiding us?' and be looking for his medals. We never knew what the medals were for. He had these medals – but we never knew what they were for or even if they were his or his father's!

Me da was a very private person and tried to bring us up to believe that your business was your business. The world and his brother didn't have to know. If we were fighting in the street he was always, 'Get them in here! Sort it out in the house! The world doesn't have to know!' We were brought up keeping everything within the confines of the house. It was, 'Nobody needs to know your business but you.'

Da was in the town one day and I don't know how many young-sters he had with him but he met this man and he hadn't seen him in a long time and the man said, 'God Willie haven't seen you in a long time. How many wains have you?' Me da told him the count was thirteen then. The man replied, 'God! Look at the grand way they've turned out!' Me da turned and he said, 'What did you expect, them to be in their bare arse because we have a whole lot of wains? We do look after them you know!'

He always said, 'I came into the world with nothing and I'll leave with not much more, but I always had my pride.' It was his belief that you might have nothing, but if you have pride you have everything.

My dad was a merchant seaman, as was his father before him. He wasn't a sailor per se, he was a boiler man. It didn't matter to him though, he sailed the world and loved it. He even lied about his age to get in. When he was fourteen he was sent out to deliver some linen and never went home. He went to the docks and the sailors made him a special shovel so he could manage the coal along with the rest of them. Our Eddie joined the Navy too for awhile but he was only in six months till home sickness brought him back. Then Jackie tried to sign up but he was just over the age limit. It was kind of a tradition in our family, but I always thought Jackie wanted to join to get away from the hassle in the army.

Jackie quit boxing about six months before Bloody Sunday. Gerry says he was tired of all the hassle he got walking down to the club and back. He had to pass through the barricades and it seems like he got a lot of grief from the soldiers. I don't know if he'd have gone back to it if he hadn't been killed. But even though he wanted to join the Merchant Navy, I think he would have because he had a great love for it.

Jackie used to go out in the morning and run around the wall round Westway and Glenowen. It was one hell of a run. I remember Jackie getting up in the morning, when he just started work. He was working for Thompson McGlinchey's. I used to walk down Westway with him, I would have headed on down to Rosemount Boys and he went on down Park Avenue. But he'd have already run twenty-five minutes around the park before he left for work.

Seems like he was always running and I'd be running after him whenever I could. Jackie delivered the papers for McCool's Shop. I went with him and my payment at the weekend was to take me down to the swimming baths or to the city picture house on Saturday. He

liked Spaghetti Westerns but he took me to see *Batman and Robin*. It wasn't like what you see now but it was a treat for me.

Treats were few and far between but we got one trip every year. We went even if it was rain, hail, or snow. My mother with her lot and my Aunt Dolly who had nine or ten of a family. They planned the day to coincide it with the 12 July because it was always said that the sun always shone on the 12 July. So the way it went was, 'Go down and ask your aunt Dolly would tomorrow be OK?' Right.

So I would run down to the next street where Dolly lived and Dolly would say, 'We will try it tomorrow, OK.' I would go back up and we started making sandwiches, packing buckets and spades, and extra coats in case it rained. The packing that went on for this day was enormous. Then all this stuff had to be carted on a bus to get this one day trip out. The bus to Buncrana was a double-decker and our two families managed to fill the top and no one else was allowed up.

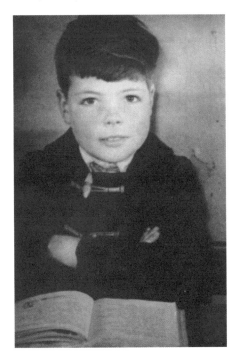

That's the way it was. Sometimes it happened that we woke on the day and it was pissing rain so I was sent back down to Dolly's to ask, 'What will we do?' The answer was always, 'Ah bugger it, the weather could pick up.' So the trip went ahead anyway, you know, regardless of what the weather was like. That was our big thing. That was our summer holiday. The rest of the time the boys went out to the fields and played football and the girls made rag dolls and played at skipping and hopscotch.

All the boys in the neighbourhood shared the one ball and one summer day me, Gerry, Liam, Jackie, and Andy were playing football. Patrick was in the house and our ball went over the wall and into the Doherty's garden. As usual, I got cheesed up to go and get the ball. I went up and was told, 'F-off! Ye're getting no ball!' I went back to the lads and reported, 'We aren't getting no ball.' Jackie said to me, 'Go over to the house and get Patrick.' The next thing I know he's over the fence and Gerry, Patrick, and Jackie are in the back garden fisticuffing over this ball. Jackie wasn't ever one to start a fight but he'd surely finish one. He soon got our ball back.

Another time we were standing over at Coyle's shop and two guys from a very tough family walked up. I mean, you just wouldn't mess with them. Jackie said to one of them, 'Were you shouting at us down the town?' The way he asked it seemed friendly enough to me, but they musn't have taken it that way because the next thing I know is Jackie tellin' them to buzz off.

The three of them squared off and Jackie put the both of them down. Big Coyle came out and said, 'What's going on here? Get away!' When Jackie came home he said, 'Thank God Johnny Coyle came out. Them boys would have kilt me!' Later Johnny Coyle drove up to the house and said, 'God young Duddy, them was two great punches!'

Kay was assigned the Christmas shopping for the wains. She always went for six pairs of trousers, six underpants, six pairs of socks, six shirts, and six jumpers at a time. The shop was on the Waterside so six sets were all she could carry at once. Then they were all tried on and this matched and that matched, and this fitted her and that fitted him, and so on. Whatever didn't fit had to be taken back to the shop and Kay started the whole process over again until everyone had one new outfit from head to toe.

Shoes were another process. My parents kept a list and you got new shoes when your name came up. There was no such thing as outgrowing them before your turn came around. We cut holes for our toes and cut out cardboard to cover our toes – you slid in the cardboard then put your foot inside. We used bits of carpet and lino sewed into them – anything to keep them together. You had to wear them until they literally fell off your feet. Then we had a go at mending the shoes ourselves. Somebody got some scrap leather and nails and you hammered it in. At one point my dad found an old shoemaker's stand and then we really got into sophisticated repairs.

Maureen was the first to get married. Seventeen people in the house (ten of them female), one bathroom, and the wedding Mass at 8.10 a.m. Kay and Bernie scrubbed all the wains the night before, and washed, ironed, and laid out their clothes. In the morning the curlers were flying and the wains getting stuck into their clothes and the rush out the door was madness.

The night before Maureen's wedding Eileen took ill. She was so sick in the morning that Kay wanted to send for a doctor, but Eileen wouldn't hear of it. This was her first wedding and she was not going to miss it. When we got back to the house after the wedding, we sent for the doctor and Eileen was rushed to hospital and had to have her appendix out. We could have killed her taking her to the wedding.

Two years later 'the big woman always in the kitchen' died. We missed her sorely but we had to get on with things too. That October Pauline would just turn four and Da needed someone to look after the household. After retiring from the Merchant Navy, Da was unemployed for a long time but at the start of that summer he'd gotten a job as a boiler man in St Columb's Hospital in the Waterside. Maureen, Kay, and Bernie were married, which left Ann as the oldest in the house. She gave up her work and took over running the house. When Ann met and married the love of her life, as luck would have it Kay's marriage broke up so she took over running the house and it just sort of moved down the line that way, whenever one moved on, another picked up the reins and ran the house till we were all raised.

Kay and Bernie always had us organised from the night before. We were scrubbed, our clothes laid out, and shoes lined up. Breakfast was tea and toast and a run out the door. The older ones took bread and jam to school and the younger ones were home for their lunch.

The boys would have you believe that it was the girls that always got into spats but if Gerry wore Jackie's shirt or Patrick's jumper there would have been a whole barney about it. There were nine girls and six boys, so in a way, we had it easy. The boys were only three to a bed but the girls were four and a half – Pauline was the half – she was so small she just jumped from bed to bed.

We fought about everything under the sun. He got more dinner than I did; I took a lend of his shoes or dirtied his jumper; she wore her knickers; he was watching something on the TV and I turned it over; I sat in his favourite chair. There were about a million things that could have started an argument. Gerry was the instigator of a lot of it. He still pushes our buttons today. Back then all you'd hear was our da shouting, 'There's not a family in this town that fights the way you crowd do! I'm sending for the priest for you!'

Our father told us to stay away from the march. Jackie went anyway. He said he was going to see his girl Bernie. Bernadette

Devlin was speaking at the march and Jackie said you could always count on good craic from Bernie. I went to play cards at Johnny Coyle's. From down in the shop I heard people yelling, 'They're murdering people down the town!' I came running up the stairs then and I seen all these boys jumping into a car and roaring off.

I went home and said, I heard our Jackie was killed down the town. My sisters gave me a hard time saying that of all my five brothers, Jackie was the least likely to get shot. Kay gave me a skite and got it out of me that I was just mouthing off. I was only carrying on, you know. An hour later the knock came at the door that Jackie was killed.

Me mammy was eighteen when she married. She died at forty-four and had fifteen children in between. Our da said he couldn't begrudge my mother one of us. That's how he came to terms with me mammy and Jackie's deaths. He said he knew why the Sacred Heart took her, she wasn't meant to be here to go through this. She wasn't meant to be alive to see one of her sons die.

Before he died, Jackie left a note for Patrick, 'Dear Patrick, I have borrowed four bob from your trouser pocket and I will give it back to you when I get paid. – Jackie.'

Since Bloody Sunday, the privacy our da treasured has been taken away. We are no longer Maureen, Bernie, Kathleen, Anne, Willie, Eddie, Susan, Eileen, Patrick, Gerry, Margaret, Theresa, Michael, and Pauline, but 'Michael, brother of Jackie Duddy killed on Bloody Sunday.' The photo of Father Daly escorting my dying brother as he was carried is something we learned to live with.

Jackie was the first to be killed on Bloody Sunday, but his is the last life-story recounted in this book. That is because Jackie's story isn't finished. It will never be finished until his name is cleared and all of the Bloody Sunday victims are vindicated. At this moment, Justice Saville is deliberating. Will he clear the names of the brothers, fathers, and husbands wounded and murdered on Bloody Sunday? Soon we will know. But no matter how the inquiry is resolved we will never stop telling Jackie's story. I hope that Jackie will never be forgotten, not because he was a Derry mother's son, but because he could have been any mother's son.

Interviews

John Nash

Linda Roddy

Patrick Nash

Tommy Hazelet

Bridget Nash

Bernard Gilmour

Gerry Doherty

Maura Young

Leo Young

Helen Young

Joe McKinney

Brian Rainey

Mary Doherty

Gerry O'hEara

Fr Patrick Donaghey

Liam Wray

Margaret Wray

Roslin Doyle

John Duddy

Bridie McDaid

Kevin McDaid

Leo Carlin

John Bradley

Eileen Doherty

Paul Doherty

Karen Carlin

Kay Duddy

Bernie Duddy

Gerry Duddy

Michael Duddy

Charlie McGuigan

Annie McKinney

Mickey McKinney

George McKinney

Ann McKinney

Kathleen McKinney

John Kelly

Ita McKinney

Kevin McKinney

Regina McKinney

Louis McKinney

Mickey Bradley

Afterword

24 MARCH 2004

It is one year and two days since I sat with Mickey McKinney in the Bloody Sunday Family Centre, he asked me to write the life stories of the victims, and I promised I would. As I write my final words, Saville deliberates. Many look to him to find the answer, the truth of Bloody Sunday. But Saville inquires only into the deaths of 30 January 1972. The Truth is in their lives. The Truth lies before that Sunday. Before these men and boys were murdered. Before their blood ran in the streets. Before their names were smeared by the press. Before they were labelled gunmen and bombers. Before Sunday, 30 January 1972, they were sons, fathers, brothers, uncles, and friends. Before Sunday, they lived.

This book would not have been possible without the generous support of the Bloody Sunday families. I feel deep affection and enormous gratitude towards these families who opened their homes and shared their lives. For a year they opened their doors and their hearts to a Yank. I was a stranger to the events of Bloody Sunday, not initially well-versed in Northern Ireland's history, and had no connection to Derry. They nonetheless spent hours telling me about their fathers, brothers, sons, and friends. It is a testament to their desire to tell the life stories of their loved ones. I feel so blessed to have met Mrs McKinney and Mrs Kelly. Who was I to be given the privilege of hearing Willie McKinney's life story from his mother? She told the story with such joy as I sat at her feet in her living room that I asked her to tell me again and again. I am grateful to have her beautiful voice on tape and I hope I have done her justice in my retelling here.

They all gave me something. Equally as treasured as sitting on Mrs McKinney's living-room floor, listening to her tell her son's story, is dining late into the night with the Gerald McKinney clan, listening to Uncle Louis' stories, joining his boisterous laugh; how I was giddy with the simple fact that I knew a short cut to the McDaid's; my feeling that I could never repay Lee Harold, Hazel Donaldson, and Ivan Cooper who were there for me every day, through thick and thin, never judging, always available, endlessly kind; Leo Carlin's insistence that I eat with him and his family's open embrace; how Kathleen Gilmour's smile and ever-ready cigarette made me feel welcome; Gerry Duddy's gruff exterior that was belied by his tenderness for his family and his engulfing bear hug; his wife Ann's fry and warm kitchen gossip; Mickey McKinney's steadfast belief that we were doing the right thing; the Nash family supper table where we hashed things out and especially Padraig who brought me chocolate; Maura Young who let me off the hook when I was human and walked me around Derry that first week making sure I had my bearings; Mary Doherty's kind smile and gentle spirit; the twinkle in Margaret Wray's eyes that must remind people of her mother; Karen Carlin *née* Doherty's raw honesty; the Kelly family's devotion to their mother; John Duddy's wink, smile, and coffee-talk; and, of course, Gerry Doherty's unwavering support and true friendship.

Bibliography

Adams, Gerry. *Free Ireland: Towards a Lasting Peace* (Roberts Rinehart: Maryland, 1994).

Adams, Gerry. *Hope and History: Making Peace in Ireland* (Brandon: Kerry, 2003).

Algren, Nelson. *The Neon Wilderness* (Peter Smith: Massachusetts, 1968).

Brunt, Stephen. *Facing Ali: The Opposition Weighs In* (Sidgwick & Jackson: London 2002).

Cahill, Thomas. *How the Irish Saved Civilization* (Anchor: New York, 1995).

Carver, (Field Marshall Lord). *Britain's Army in the Twentieth Century* (Macmillan: London,1999).

Ciccone, F. Richard. *Royko: A Life in Print* (Public Affairs: New York, 2001).

Connolly, S.J. *The Oxford Company to Irish History* (Oxford University Press, 1998).

Coogan, Tim Pat. *The Troubles: Ireland's Ordeal and the Search for Peace* (Arrow: London, 1995).

Cunningham, Phillip. *Derry Down the Days* (Guildhall: Derry, 2002).

Daly, Edward. *Mister, Are You a Priest?* (Four Courts: Dublin, 2000).

Dash, Samuel. *Justice Denied: A Challenge to Lord Widgery's Report on 'Bloody Sunday'* (International League for the Rights of Man: New York, 1998).

Day, Angelique and McWilliams, Patrick, eds. *Ordance Survey: Memoirs of Ireland. Vol. 27 Parishes of Co. London Derry VIII 1830, 1833-7, 1839* (Dufour: Pennsylvania, 1994).

Dillion, Martin, *The Shankill Butchers* (Hutchinson: London, 1989).

Doherty, Paddy & Hegarty, Peter. *Paddy Bogside* (Mercier: Cork, 2001).

Foster, R.F. *The Irish Story Telling Tales and Making it Up in Ireland* (Allen Lane: London, 2001).

Graham, Katherine. *Personal History* (Vintage: New York, 1998).

Grimaldi, Fulvio & North, Susan. *Blood in the Streets* (Guildhall: Derry, 1998).

Holland, Jack. *Hope Against History: The Course of Conflict in Northern Ireland* (Hodder & Stoughton: London, 1999).

Hume, John. *A New Ireland: Politics, Peace, and Reconciliation* (Roberts Rinehart: Maryland, 1997).

Hume, John. *Derry Beyond the Walls: Social and Economics Aspects of the Growth Derry 1825-1850* (Ulster Historical foundation: Belfast, 2002).

Keneally, John. *The Great Shame and the Triumph of the Irish in the English-Speaking*

World (Doubleday: New York, 1998).

Lacey, Brian. *City of Derry* (Cottage Publications: Donaghadee, 1995).

MacDonald, Michael Patrick. *All Souls: A Family Story from Southie* (Beacon: Massachusetts, 1999).

McCann, Eamonn. *Bloody Sunday in Derry: What Really Happened* (Brandon: Kerry, 2000).

McCann, Eamonn. *War and an Irish Town* (Pluto: London, 1993).

McConnell, Seamus. *The Ultimate Wile: Big Derry Phrasebook* (Guildhall: Derry, 2001).

McKittrick, David, et al. *Lost Lives* (Mainstream: Edinburgh, 1999).

McMahon, Sean. *The Derry Anthology* (Blackstaff: Belfast, 2002).

McSheffrey, Gerald. *Planning Derry: Planning and Politics in Northern Ireland* (Liverpool University Press, 2000).

Moloney, Ed. *A Secret History of the IRA* (W.W. Norton: New York, 2002).

Mullan, Don. *Eyewitness Bloody Sunday* (Wolfhound: Dublin, 1999).

O'Dochartaigh Niall. *From Civil Rights to Armalites: Derry and the Birth of the Irish Troubles* (Cork University Press, 1997).

Royko, Mike. *One More Time* (University of Chicago Press, 1999).

Taylor, Peter. *Brits: The War Against the IRA* (Bloomsbury: London, 2001).

Taylor, Peter. *Loyalists* (TV Books: New York, 1999).

Terkel, Studs. *Division Street America* (New Press: New York, 1993).

Terkel, Studs. *'The Good War': An Oral History of World War II* (Pantheon: New York, 1984).

The Bogside Artists. *Murals* (Guildhall: Derry, 2001).

Walsh, Dermot. *Bloody Sunday and the Rule of Law in Northern Ireland* (Gill & Macmillan: Dublin, 2000).

Walsh, Dermot. *The Bloody Sunday Tribunal of Inquiry: A Resounding Defeat for Truth, Justice and the Rule of Law* (Bloody Sunday Trust: Derry, 1999).

Endnotes

BACKGROUND TO BLOODY SUNDAY

1   The Parachute Regiment, www.parachute-regiment.co.uk.
2   The names of the soldiers have not been released by the British Government.
3   Soldier 027, 1 Para, Anti-Tank Plt.
4   The Apprentice Boys are a Protestant fraternity, founded in 1814 to commemo-
    rate the 1688 Siege of Derry, when 13 apprentice boys closed the city gates
    against the army of Catholic King James.
5   *Marching On*. Exhibition Catalogue of Gasyard Wall Feile 2003. Opening
    Statement of Queen's Council Christopher Clarke to the Bloody Sunday
    Inquiry, 27 March 2000.
6   Jack Holland, 41.
7   Field Marshall Lord Carver.
8   Walsh, *Bloody Sunday and the Rule of Law in Northern Ireland*, 40.
9   Special Powers Act, conferring RUC duties to British soldiers and Northern
    Ireland (Emergency Provisions) Act 1973.

JOHNNY JOHNSTON

10   John Duddy.
11   The Bloody Sunday Inquiry Transcript of Proceedings 132: 13-16, 25: 133:1
     (Monday, 24 November 2003, Day 400).
12   Medical record of John Johnston. Royal Victoria Hospital, Belfast. May 1972.
13   *Bloody Sunday and the Report of the Widgery Tribunal: The Irish Government's
     Assessment of the New Material*, para. 146, 79 quoting Don Mullan, Eyewitness
     Bloody Sunday, The Truth 86 (1997).
14   The Bloody Sunday victims were shot with 7.62mm (high-velocity) rounds.
15   Letter of January 1972, titled 'The Situation in Londonderry as at 7th January
     1972 from General Ford to GOC'.
16   Northern Ireland Civil Rights Association.
17   Letter of 26 January 1998 from Frank Lagan to the *Irish News*.
18   Confirmatory Notes to Oral Orders given by Co 1 R Anglican at Ebrington at
     291000 Z, Jan 1972

JIM WRAY

19 Margaret Wray.
20 Margaret Wray.
21 Statement of Joe Mahon to Saville Inquiry, 17 September 1999.

GERARD MCKINNEY

22 Kevin McKinney.
23 Statement of John O'Kane to the Bloody Sunday Inquiry, 12 May 1999.

JOHN YOUNG

24 Lily Young.

GERALD DONAGHEY

25 Widgery, Paragraph 84.
26 Walsh, 'The Bloody Sunday Tribunal of Inquiry: A Resounding Defeat for Truth, Justice, and the Rule of Law', 51.

MICHAEL KELLY

27 Mrs Alex (Bridget) Nash.
28 One child died in infancy.
29 Mrs Kelly died 21 June 2004.

WILLIAM MCKINNEY

30 Notes from RUC investigation into Bloody Sunday. Sealed but not dated.
31 Mrs McKinney died 16 July 2005.

WILLIAM NASH

32 John P. Coyle, *Down the Quay*, 18 (1990).
33 *Ibid.*, 20.

MICHAEL MCDAID

34 Bridie Gallagher, Michael's sister.
35 Leo Carlin.

PADDY DOHERTY

[36] Eileen Doherty.
[37] Statement of Leo Carlin to Bloody Sunday Inquiry, 6 October 1998.
[38] Walsh, *Bloody Sunday and the Rule of Law in Northern Ireland*, 210.

JACKIE DUDDY

[39] Gerry Duddy.